ADVENTURES
WITH OLLIE

ADVENTURES WITH OLLIE

By

Adrian Chamberlain

OOLICHAN BOOKS
FERNIE, BRITISH COLUMBIA, CANADA
2012

Library and Archives Canada Cataloguing in Publication

Chamberlain, Adrian, 1958-

    Adventures with Ollie / Adrian Chamberlain.

ISBN 978-0-88982-291-7

    1. Chamberlain, Adrian, 1958-. 2. Pug--Anecdotes.

3. Dog owners--Anecdotes. 4. Authors, Canadian (English)--

21st century--Biography. I. Title.

SF429.P9C53 2012   636.76   C2012-905744-4

We gratefully acknowledge the financial support of the Canada Council for the Arts, the British Columbia Arts Council through the BC Ministry of Tourism, Culture, and the Arts, and the Government of Canada through the Canada Book Fund, for our publishing activities.

Published by
Oolichan Books
P.O. Box 2278
Fernie, British Columbia
Canada V0B 1M0

www.oolichan.com

Printed in Canada

To Penny and Katie.
And my mother Audrey …
who always enjoys a good laugh.

CONTENTS

A PUG FALLS IN VICTORIA

My wife didn't want us to buy a dog at first. Too much trouble. Too much fuss.

"We'll get one when you're retired," she said.

"But by then I'll be a miserable old man," I said.

"All the better. You can cheer yourself up in your twilight years by taking it for long healthful walks."

I was persistent in my quest, having always wanted a dog. And, thanks to my formidable powers of persuasion (me saying "I want a pug dog" over and over) we acquired Ollie the Pug 18 months ago.

Our introduction to the joys of pug-dog ownership got off to a rough start. When we first visited Ollie the Pug's breeders, something unpleasant happened.

All the pug pups were frolicking in the breeders' living room. They looked like miniature furry pigs. The pugs, I mean. Irresistible. I picked one up. As it sat in my lap, the pup squirmed in a tremendously athletic manner. It fell, hitting its head on the hardwood floor. It sounded like a felt-covered coconut colliding with a gymnasium floor.

The poor little tyke stood up, shook itself and wobbled off. It looked slightly unsteady, in the manner of someone disembarking after an especially harrowing ocean voyage.

Silence descended upon the room. A clock ticked

loudly. Outside, the faint cries of street urchins were audible. I imagined I could hear daffodil bulbs pushing their tender green tips through spring-kissed soil.

The pup's owners, a young man and wife, exchanged an ambiguous look. Dropping puppies on floors is, of course, a heinous social faux pas. Not quite as bad as drinking five martinis, dancing vigorously to ABBA and vomiting on the rug, but worse than telling an off-colour joke at a dinner party.

"Sorry," I said.

"Yeah," said the young man.

"Dog squirmed," I added awkwardly. "Hard to hold."

I waited for the breeders to say, "Look, bud. We sell dogs only to good owners. Not sausage-fingered clods who catapult defenceless pugs on their still-soft heads."

"Well ..." said the breeder's wife. "That's OK."

We agreed to take possession of Ollie the Pug in 10 days, after weaning. On the drive home, my wife said, "Boy. That was lucky."

I turned to look at her.

"The pug you dropped wasn't a male. And it's a male that we're buying."

What a happy thought! When I was 13, my dad bought a brand new 1971 Toyota sedan. Two minutes out of the car lot, he was T-boned by a drunk guy who'd run a stop sign. A post-accident car never seems the same, even after it's repaired. I imagine the same rule applies to pug dogs.

The sun was setting, a blood-red ball on the horizon. Oh yes, life was pretty good, after all.

DAWN RELIEF FORAY ENDS
IN BRIEFS ENCOUNTER

When we first got Ollie the Pug, I'd escort him outside each morning to relieve himself. This was part of the pug-ownership pact made with my wife—a solemn promise on my part.

When Ollie was a wee pup, this task meant rising at 6 a.m. daily. Apparently, pug pups have pea-sized bladders and cannot retain their water until a civilized hour.

Getting up that early is horrible and unnatural. However, as is my habit in all things, I tried to make it easier for myself.

At first, I'd dress completely before taking Ollie into the front yard. But after a few days, my routine changed. It seemed easier to simply throw a raincoat over my pyjamas, slip on some unfashionable crocs and stumble out.

And then, to make things really easy, I started wearing just a raincoat, crocs and a pair of Y-front underpants. Nothing else. The raincoat hid my state of undress. Well, partially. And our front yard is almost hidden from the street by trees.

Typically, Ollie would bite leaves and lick grass blades instead of doing his duty. On one such occasion I gazed upwards, toward the heavens, feeling the splash of raindrops on my face. At that precise moment, I felt ... well, under surveillance. I turned my head and noticed our neighbour staring at me from her balcony.

(Let me make it clear this was our old neighbour. Not the new neighbour who might read this and become annoyed. The old neighbour was a woman who habitually sat on her balcony to yak on her cellphone. This happened daily, and was horribly vexing.)

"Hi," I said to this neighbour. She was still gripping her cellphone, but now—for the first time ever—was not talking into it.

She said nothing to me. The cellphone lady had noted my bare legs and underwear. She likely pegged me as a flasher or some other undesirable. I began to wish my raincoat was considerably longer. Say, three-quarters length.

My neighbour and I had previously had an awkward, wordless encounter. One sunny summer day, I decided to recline on a chaise-lounge on our balcony. I wore only a pair of Y-fronts. It was, after all, a hot day. And this particular balcony is at the back of our house, very high up, off our bedroom. Pretty private—or so I imagined.

Unfortunately, as I read, my wife—not noticing my presence—locked the french doors to the balcony before driving off to undertake a marathon shopping trip. This left me alone, in my underpants, locked out. I banged on the french doors.

"Let me in," I yelled. "I'm in my underwear here!"

Sadly my wife was half-way to Wal-Mart. However, the noise did attract the notice of the cellphone lady next door. She regarded me from her balcony with a solemn expression, as though viewing some much-vaunted tourist attraction that had proved utterly disappointing.

"Wife locked me out," I said to her, smiling and shielding myself with a dog-eared copy of *Sons and Lovers*. She said nothing.

"That's why I'm in my underwear," I said. "Ordinarily, I'm fully clothed."

Fortunately, my Y-fronts were clean and in good repair. If I'd worn my tattered pair, she might have phoned 911.

Back to the present. There I was in the yard with Ollie, who was vigorously biting a stick instead of relieving himself. I locked eyes again with my neighbour, who seemed unable to avert her gaze. Possibly she was recalling me as the protagonist in the infamous *Sons and Lovers* incident.

Then I heard clinking at the front gate. The old man who steals refundable bottles from our recycling boxes was foraging in our blue box once again. He, too, stared at my outfit.

"How's it going?" I said cheerfully. He said nothing. What a peculiar day this was shaping up to be.

Finally, Ollie lifted his hind leg and let fly. Thank God. Meanwhile, the cellphone lady scurried back into her home, no doubt keen to report a half-naked man cavorting in his yard.

Now, when venturing outside, I am always fully dressed. Well … pyjama-clad, at the very least.

OLLIE SPARKS POSITIVE
BEHAVIOURAL CHANGE

Ollie the Pug is forcing me to be a more pleasant person. This is good, I suppose.

Then again, it makes me feel like someone who has infiltrated the ranks of Up With People under false pretenses.

We recently took Ollie on vacation to Gabriola Island. It was amazing how many people approached us to pat him and have a chat.

This happens sometimes during his walks around our Saanich neighbourhood. But on Gabriola—brimming with tourists in a happy holiday mood—these incidents were pretty well constant. There would be as many as a dozen Ollie stop-and-chats every day.

How nice, you might say. Perhaps. But these Ollie-related encounters put me in a new and unaccustomed role, that of Mr. Nice Guy.

You see, I'm not really that nice of a person. Ask my friends, my colleagues, my family. While not absolutely evil—like Pol Pot or the scary dentist from *Marathon Man*—I will chuckle frequently at the misfortunes of others. If someone slips on a discarded candy wrapper or suffers a minor auto accident while conversing on their cellphone, I laugh freely and heartily. Of course, when the tables are turned—when someone takes pleasure in my misfortunes—I fail to see the humour and wonder how people can be so heartless and cruel.

But when approached for an Ollie the Pug pat-'n'-chat, I always feel compelled to be affable. Not sure why. It feels odd, like wearing an item of clothing I'd ordinarily never wear. Perhaps culottes or a colourful hat made from boiled wool.

"Why does your dog's tongue stick out?" a little red-haired girl asked me. I was sitting with Ollie in front of a grocery store on Gabriola.

My first thought was, "How on earth would I know? Now buzz off, little girl, so I can enjoy lounging in the sun while my wife fetches me a tall cappuccino."

What I said was, "Oh, I think it's because Ollie's tongue is too long. Do you want to pet him? Sure, go ahead. Don't be scared. He's a friendly puppy."

Minutes later, a 20-something woman with army pants, a dyed-blond crewcut and a Rosie the Riveter tattoo stopped in front of me.

"Oh. Cute. Cute. Your dog is cute. Don't you think he's cute? I have a boxer at home."

My first thought was, "Who cares about your boxer? Don't touch Ollie. He's scared of your tattoo."

What I said was, "Awww. A boxer? Those are great dogs. Hey … have a super day."

A super day? Who was I, for God's sake? Kelly Ripa?

The kicker, though, was encountering a gaggle of middle-aged folk practising yoga at Twin Beaches Park. I suspect they were on the island to participate in horrible personal development courses in which one learns to become "fully alive" and engage in healthy relationships.

The yoga people were being instructed by a guy in tight white shorts. He was saying things like, "Now let's repulse the monkey."

As Ollie and I strolled by, they took a break. Then they surrounded us. I became alarmed, in case they decided to favour us with a group hug.

Instead, the yogists took turns caressing Ollie lovingly.

"How old is he?" they asked. "What's his name? Isn't he a good little dog?"

I told them Ollie's name and age. I agreed that he is, indeed, a good little dog. And I wished these wretched yogists a good, pleasant afternoon.

Could it be Ollie is forcing me to become a nicer person?

I shudder to think.

WHEN PUGS
PARTY HEARTY

Ollie the Pug went to his first party recently. It was a birthday party. He went absolutely bonkers.

Ironically, the woman hosting the party had specifically requested Ollie's presence. "I don't think that's such a good idea," I said on the phone. At that moment, Ollie was biting a squeaky toy and moaning loudly.

"Why not?" she asked. "Who's that doing all the moaning?"

"Because he will gobble up all the food and—if he becomes overly excited—possibly relieve himself on your nice new carpet."

She thought I was joking. And so it came to be that Ollie was duly outfitted with his fake bow-tie collar (purchased by my wife for those oh-so-special occasions) and packed off in the Volvo.

Ollie the Pug is always tremendously excited at the prospect of a car ride. The word "car" sends him into paroxysms of delight, causing him to leap around like a rabbit and make strangulated yelps. Yet once inside the car, he behaves like a condemned man who, having been flung into a metal cell, now awaits news of his execution. Ollie runs about unhappily and whines, pressing his muzzle to the window.

"Well, should be good times at the party," I said, drumming my fingers on the steering wheel.

My wife grinned. She was all happy because Ollie was wearing his bow tie, which—due to his fat neck—makes him look like a chubby butler.

As we expected, Ollie behaved like a crazy pug dog at this afternoon event. Not terrible, but you really had to keep your eye on him at all times.

It made me wonder, what if we all behaved like Ollie the Pug at parties?

Upon entering, you would greet each guest by licking them and wiggling your posterior with vigour. You would almost certainly sniff the bottoms of other guests. You would definitely dash around the kitchen a few times, sniffing the air.

Each time a fellow guest ate something—say a pickle or a gobbet of brie—you would stare at them intently. Your eyes would follow their fingers with the dedicated gaze of a jeweller contemplating the Hope Diamond. You would have zero use for conversation. For you would be on a single-minded quest, that is, to consume as much food as possible.

If no one was looking, you would attempt to climb onto the table containing all of the food. Other guests would tell you "no!" Some might call even you a "bad boy!" But you would be oblivious to such admonishments, because—you know—there's a whole bunch of food on the table.

Several times, because of your excitement at being in close proximity to people and food, you would leap up on the host's newly upholstered velvet couches. You would shove your head into the crack between the cushions, and make snortling noises. You might also shove your nose into the crotches of surprised and not always delighted guests.

When this excitement paled, you would dash into the bathroom and take refreshing gulps of cool water from the toilet. Then you would go into the host's bedroom, somehow find her silk pyjamas under her pillow, and commence biting these pyjamas. And then it would be back to the toilet for more refreshment. Because biting other people's pyjamas is terribly thirsty work.

Finally, excited by the sounds of voices and the smells of various cheeses, you would engage in a pug run.

This means dashing around the house in circles, at a fever pitch, over and over. After five minutes of this, you would lie down in the middle of the living room with your tongue out. And then you would fall asleep.

Then someone would awaken you by saying, "OK. Let's go. Wanna go in the car?"

And yes, you would want to go into the car! Yet once inside the car you would become terribly maudlin, weeping and whining while pressing your face to the window.

At least, that's how it was for Ollie the Pug at his first party.

DOO AS YOU
WOULD BE DONE BY

Does it strike anyone else as strange that we dog owners must pick up our pets' droppings?

It seems so, well … demeaning.

This practice is, of course, mandatory in urban areas. How different from Gabriola Island, where I grew up. Dogs defecated boldly and freely as they scampered over hill and vale, chasing sheep and dodging the occasional shotgun blast delivered by angry farmers. Oh, what a merry life they led!

In Victoria, by contrast, we dutifully trudge behind our pets, biodegradable plastic bags at the ready. When our dog starts walking in that telltale circle, we swoop in like trained falcons for retrieval. Then we hold our bag aloft—oh joy!— as though we've snagged the rarest of truffles.

If a space alien observed my own biodegradable bag antics, he'd assume Ollie the Pug was king and I his humble manservant. After all, what task could be more menial?

What if the tables were turned? Golly, I'd love to roam the streets, defecating freely, with some peon to scoop up behind me. "Good boy! Good boy!" my servant would declare, offering me a reward (not a doggie treat, but a small glass of Talisker). And I'd down my scotch in a single gulp, thinking, "You know … I *am* a good boy!"

This brings to mind an incident from a few months ago. I took Ollie the Pug out for a walk. The sun shone, cherry trees bloomed, a breeze whispered sweet nothings.

At a grassy corner, Ollie stopped and sniffed. Sensing my cue, I seized my biodegradable plastic bag.

False alarm. Ollie had discovered a stray french fry, which he began to devour. At that moment, a woman turning the corner in her SUV yelled at me.

"Hey, you! I hope you're picking up your dog's poop! Because, you know, you should be picking that up! The friggin' poop I mean!"

Her manner was distinctly unfriendly, as though I'd been lopping off the heads of her prize tulips with a walking stick.

"Don't worry!" I said, producing my biodegradable bag and holding it for her to see. Then I stopped short. Why should I offer such a churlish person proof of my good and neighbourly intentions?

The woman pulled into her driveway. It was clear she lived on the property adjoining the grassy knoll. No doubt neighbourhood dogs were routinely using this corner for a latrine. Perhaps, once or twice, this unpleasant person had squashed doggie doo under her unfashionable Crocs.

Fair enough. But to publicly upbraid a law-abiding citizen such as myself; why, it seemed terribly unjust. After all, I'm constantly retrieving Ollie's droppings. If there was a contest for this sort of thing, I'd be declared the all-time champion of my neighbourhood. Or at least first runner up.

Ollie and I continued our walk in the park. He did his business. I dutifully retrieved it with my biodegradable plastic bag.

On the way home, a plan began to formulate in my mind. As we strolled past the yelling lady's house, I flung Ollie's poo bag into her driveway. Ha! Talk about poetic justice. Some sort of moral victory was surely mine.

At home, I told my wife the tale of the lady and the biodegradable poo bag. But instead of embracing me with an admiring, "Oh, well done!" she merely said, "Uh-oh."

"What?" I said.

"Well … it just sounds a little juvenile. I mean, that's just a really silly thing to do."

Damn. Then I heard a sound from the couch. Heavy snoring. It was Ollie the Pug. Oblivious. But you know, it looked like he was smiling.

NOT FAT, PERHAPS
A LITTLE COBBY

Ollie the Pug got into trouble recently.

I'd awakened at my usual time, which is now (depressingly) 6 a.m. This gives me time to take Ollie into the backyard to relieve himself before I start work. The blare of the early morning alarm clock is horrific, perhaps the aural equivalent of having hot cattle-brands thrust into your eyes while listening to Celine Dion's "The Power of Love" through headphones super-glued to your ears.

But I digress.

After Ollie's backyard visit, I decided to return to bed to get some extra shut-eye. Sleep wouldn't return, though. Once you're up, you're up, I guess. Besides, I could hear curious noises coming from the living room.

I got out of bed, encountering my wife at the bedroom door. She wore a worried expression.

"Ollie is stuck under the chest of drawers," she said. "He can't get out."

It was true. Ollie had inserted himself under this heavy piece of furniture, and was making frantic chortling noises. In the past, when seized with the urge to crawl under the chest of drawers, he had always been able to lie on his side and struggle out. But now he's too fat.

To make the chest lighter, in order to lift it and facilitate pug release, we had to pull out all the drawers. During this process, Ollie whimpered and scrabbled frantically with his paws. We finally lifted, and Ollie zoomed out, like a cork popping from a bottle of Asti. He appeared to grin, assuming the cocky attitude of the insufferable David Blaine after a particularly amazing escape trick.

Lest any pet owners become perturbed, let me assure your that Ollie the Pug is about the right weight. He weighs 87 lbs. No, just kidding. He is 23 lbs. For a larger pug, that's considered not too bad. And our vet noted Ollie has a "defined waist," which is vet code for "Your dog, he tips the scales real good but he sure ain't no great big porker."

I think the technical term for such a pug is "cobby." He's compact and stubby. What a great word cobby is. How useful in daily discourse.

For instance, when your mother-in-law points out the circumference of your waist as you request a second helping of triple-fudge cheesecake, one need only respond, "Allay your fears, beloved relative, for I am not overweight, but merely cobby."

Anyway, back to Ollie. To be perfectly truthful, our vet did say he is about a pound overweight.

I blame the cheese sandwich for this state of affairs.

Some time ago, there was a crackling noise in the front room. More of a shredding noise, really. My wife found Ollie, who had ripped apart her paper lunch bag and discovered a cheddar cheese sandwich. Ollie was gobbling it down with the zeal of an IRA hunger-striker breaking a 30-day fast.

"Bad dog, Ollie, bad dog," I said, which of course to any dog sounds like, "Blah-de-blah, Ollie, blah-de-blah."

We decided to put Ollie on a diet, so he could lose the pound. No more snacks. More walks. After a few weeks, he was back at the vet for a routine shot. So we weighed Ollie again. Twenty-three pounds.

Hadn't lost an ounce.

We have rolled up some horrible place mats someone once gave us (they have the thickness and consistency of yoga mats) under the chest of drawers to keep Ollie out. Meanwhile, the diet/exercise regime continues.

POTTY TRAINING
A PUG IS TOUGH

Apparently, pug dogs are more difficult to house-train than most breeds. Sadly, during my pre-purchase research, this crucial info-nugget was somehow overlooked.

After we adopted Ollie the Pug, he defecated freely all over the house. This continued for months. He relieved himself with what one, in the old days, might term "gay abandon." Or with what, in the new days, one might call "no regard for carpets."

It was only around the 14-month mark that Ollie began to grapple with such weighty concepts as "Potty" and "Is it time to go outside?" and "Not on the carpet" and "What? On the carpet again?"

Don't get me wrong. Ollie the Pug is a nice pet. He has a super personality: friendly, outgoing, non-biting (usually). But if he'd come with the appropriate warning sticker— "Will pepper your home with turds for an entire year or more"—I might have considered a goldfish.

For me, the capper was our new Turkish rug. I've always wanted one. Finally, I located the perfect Turkish rug online. The colours were fantastic. Muted, not gaudy.

"I'm going to buy this cool and tasteful Turkish rug," I told my wife.

"Is that a good idea?" she said. "Don't forget about that funny shirt you bought."

She meant a shirt I'd acquired online. It looked good in the picture. Sadly, when it arrived, it turned out to be much too small. Apparently, with this particular company, size large means: "For the tiny man, possibly living with dwarfism or equivalent." I looked like a sausage in this shirt. It went to the Salvation Army.

The rug finally arrived. I was worried, in case the colours didn't match the photo. Oh, happy day. Everything was good. For once, victory was mine.

What I'd forgotten was the pug-dog factor. The first Ollie-the-Pug offering was discovered by accident. I walked onto the new, Scotch-guarded rug in my bare feet, only to encounter something squishy. Lodged between my toes was an object the size of a half-smoked cigarillo.

Only, you know … it was no cigarillo.

Despite my pleadings, Ollie has used the Turkish rug as a latrine numerous times. Compounding the problem is the rug's dense pattern, making turd detection a Where's Waldo?-type challenge.

It wasn't just the new rug, though. Ollie would let fly in the kitchen, the upstairs study, the basement, the computer room. It seemed every time you took your eyes off Ollie, he was scampering off to pinch a mini-loaf in some obscure nook.

I became so paranoid, every time Ollie the Pug walked in a circle (a sure tip-off) I'd swoop down, tuck him in the crook of my arm and sprint to the door like Super Joe Montana.

Friends and colleagues all advised "crating" to speed up house-training. Essentially, crating means caging dogs in a tiny plastic prison. The notion is that they prefer not to defecate where they live. Ultimately, then, the crate becomes a turd-free zone.

Ollie has a crate. But he doesn't like being in it. And I don't like imprisoning him. It seems cruel. So instead, we persevered with conventional house-training, which progressed at snail-like pace.

Not to sound obsessed or anything, but I must tell you about Ollie's most spectacular bowel movement. This occurred during a Romper School class. Romper School is a weekly doggie class, in which pups run around like maniacs in a gymnasium. The theory is, they learn to socialize. Ollie loves it.

Near the end of one class, Ollie ran to the middle of the room. For some reason, it became deathly quiet. All eyes were upon him. Ollie then squatted and indulged in his favourite activity. And then—get this—he started to grin. No kidding.

One Rover Romper Room staffer trudged over with mop and bucket as the other announced brightly, "OK everyone. Looks like Romper School is over!"

Happily, most of these memories are subsiding. Ollie has been good for a few months now. And I've had the Turkish rug cleaned. Looks like new. Well, almost.

POTTY BELL FAILS TO TOLL

It seems Ollie the Pug ought to be fully potty-trained by now. He's now 18 months old, surely beyond the puppy stage.

But, in the words of Elvis Costello, accidents will happen.

I'd say Ollie is 98 per cent house-trained. When things go awry, eating seems to function as a trigger. After he has gobbled either of his two daily meals, I regard Ollie the Pug as a loaded gun, ready to explode on my new Turkish rug.

If Ollie does anything in our house resembling a circle-shaped march, I frog-walk him to the door quicker than Jessica Simpson getting ejected from a Mensa convention.

My wife read that it's a terrific idea to buy your dog a set of bells. Experts say some dogs (no doubt the civilized sort who wear smoking jackets and ascots) will ring their bells to politely indicate it's potty-time, and that they prefer to relieve themselves outdoors.

So we bought a set of bells on a string, hanging them near the front door.

"Look Ollie," my wife would say. "Ring those bells when you need to go potty."

My wife would then ring the potty-bells. And Ollie would stare at her, his face blank and uncomprehending.

He brought to mind a particularly dim basketball player from my high-school algebra class who, on occasion, would be called upon by a sadistic teacher to stand up and solve a problem.

Our dog never rang his potty-bells. Not once. I suggested these bells be reinstalled beside my bed. I imagined activating them on late Sunday mornings, so family members might serve me breakfast in bed. This suggestion went over poorly, however.

Several months ago, my wife discovered Ollie the Pug had used the upstairs futon as a secret urinal.

"Look at this mattress," she said, making me look. Not a pretty sight.

Of course, it all added up. Prior to this horrific discovery, our daughter's boyfriend sometimes used the futon to take naps. When my daughter informed him of Ollie's stunt, he said, "Oh. That makes sense. Because that futon didn't smell so good."

My wife hired a guy to steam-clean our futon mattress. She did this against my wishes, as I believed the urine-encrusted mattress ought to be destroyed, preferably in a raging bonfire surrounding by chanting witches waving incense sticks.

But she assured me a good steam-clean would remove the odour and stains. And by golly, it did.

And there was more good news. Ollie stopped using the futon as a latrine. It appeared victory was well within our grasp. That is, until we had a house guest.

My brother-in-law, who's from Nanaimo, stayed overnight because he wanted to get up early for a sailboat race out of Victoria. After he left to go boating, my wife went upstairs to change the futon sheets. Horror of horrors—Ollie the Pug had defecated on the futon.

"Perhaps he's attempting to mark out his territory after detecting an unfamiliar scent," I suggested helpfully.

My wife, busy removing this fresh evidence, looked at me—but said nothing.

"At least your brother wasn't on the futon at the time," I added. More silence.

Happily, Ollie the Pug has been good ever since the sailboat race incident. (Or as I now call it, *l'incident de course de voilier.*)

On a final note, a word of advice: If my wife ever offers you the upstairs futon for a sleep-over, I'd weigh my options very, very carefully.

PUZZLED POOCH ENDURES
THE HALLOWEEN BUZZ

Just before Halloween, my wife said she needed to buy a bee costume. You know, for Ollie the Pug.

Ollie really, really wanted to dress up as a bee for Halloween. At least, that's what my wife told me.

"Either that," she said, "or a ladybug."

So we went to London Drugs, where it turned out my wife had—during a previous covert operation—sussed out the Halloween costumes. In fact, Ollie's costume was in a rack for little kids.

"I just need to cut off the arms," said my wife, holding a bee costume aloft. "I really think this will work."

As we walked over to the cashier, a middle-aged woman in electric-blue sweat pants stared at us. Then she barked, "Adorable bee costume!"

"Thanks," said my wife, beaming.

The cashier, a young woman, examined the bee costume. Then she told us the toddler pictured on the label looks a lot like her daughter.

"I bet she'd look good in this bee costume," said my wife.

"You got that right," said the cashier.

Upon returning home, my wife sprinted to the kitchen.

She seized a pair of scissors and commenced altering the bee costume with gusto. Ollie the Pug, meanwhile, kept trying to jump up and bite it. That's because the bee costume has feathers on it. Not sure why. Bees don't have feathers.

Then she stuffed Ollie into his bee costume. It's quite tight. Ollie is plumper than your garden-variety toddler. The bee costume has wings and a thingy for the head with two antennae sticking up. At the end of each antenna is a ball of yellow feathers.

"He looks adorable," declared my wife.

My daughter walked in.

"Aw," she said.

Ollie, meanwhile, seemed calm. But he looked puzzled. No doubt he was thinking, "What am I doing in a bee costume? I'm not a bee."

On Halloween day, my wife wanted to visit Bark & Fitz to buy dog supplies. She put Ollie in his bee costume.

At the store, Ole—the owner—greeted us. He said he liked Ollie's bee costume. And he said his pug dog, Elvis, also had a bee costume for Halloween. Apparently, it's some kind of trend. He said he'd insert Elvis into his bee costume so we could get a group shot.

"Elvis doesn't like wearing his bee costume," added Ole. Sure enough, when Elvis had it on, he looked depressed, like a guy who thought he'd won the lottery but then discovered he was one number off.

A woman in the store with a big dog—I think it was a setter or a retriever—looked at Ollie.

"Is that a girl dog?" she said.

I forgot to mention part of Ollie's bee costume is a tutu.

I guess it wasn't designed by an entomologist. We told her that Ollie, despite his appearance, is a boy dog. The woman seemed surprised by this, perhaps believing that cross-dressing of dogs is a no-no. Her big dog wasn't wearing a Halloween costume.

Around 7 p.m., my wife decided it was time to take Ollie trick-or-treating. She carried Ollie from house to house because she was worried he would urinate in his bee costume.

This sounds slightly insane, but it is actually sensible. You see, Ollie never urinates when someone is carrying him.

The first house was our next-door neighbours'. Their young children ran up to pet the tutu-wearing bee dog. Ollie licked them delightedly.

At the second (and final) house, Ollie was rewarded with a special trick-or-treat bag.

The bag included cheese hearts, milk bones and little dried fish from Chinatown. The latter made Ollie go absolutely bonkers with delight.

As I write this, on Sunday morning, Ollie is snoozing on the couch next to me. His bee costume lies rumpled on the floor. He looks like a guy who's gone on a three-day bender. Except that instead of whiskey, his breath smells like fish.

A DEDICATED
FOLLOWER OF FASHION

Being Ollie the Pug's manservant means experiencing many new things.

Take walks, for example. Not to sound lazy, but I was never one for recreational walking. I prefer to laze on the couch with a beaker of inexpensive plonk while watching *Say Yes to the Dress* or *Dancing With the Stars*.

But Ollie requires two walkies a day. So I'm regularly frog-walked around the neighbourhood, with Ollie yanking determinedly at his tether.

Last week, thanks to Ollie, I had the opportunity to be a fashion model—another first. An upscale Victoria's menswear store, Outlooks for Men, hosted the Man and His Dog fashion show. Both of us were invited to participate.

Naturally I said yes, as the event raises money for a worthy cause: Turtle Gardens Animal Rescue. But as the event drew near, I grew nervous. The notion of awkwardly strutting the catwalk in fancy duds filled me with dismay. And there was no telling what antics Ollie might pull off in a crowded room containing other dogs.

He would doubtless go absolutely bonkers, engaging in an animated chase-me-Charlie with the other hounds. I also had visions of Ollie cheerfully voiding his bowels as horrified fashionistas clasped lavender-scented hankies to their noses.

The preliminary to the fashion show was a clothes fitting. A nice woman called Vanessa outfitted me in a purple Altea shirt with matching purple scarf, which isn't my usual sort of thing. I also slipped on a black Zegna peacoat, which I liked because it sort of made me look like a pirate.

"Have you ever modelled before?" asked Vanessa. This made me bark with buccaneer laughter, although I'm sure she was just being polite.

As instructed, all men and dogs arrived early on the evening of the fashion show. The first order of business was a practice stroll on the catwalk with your pooch before the audience arrived.

Ollie was too small to climb up the steps, so I unceremoniously hoisted him up like a sack of rice. He immediately become entangled in his leash. Help was required to sort him out. Then Ollie embarked on a tug-of-war up the catwalk with me in tow, making both dog and owner look slightly demented. This did not bode well.

The dogs were ushered into a separate room while the men changed downstairs. The change room was communal. That's something I'm not crazy about. The sole reason I hate public swimming pools is because of the communal change room. Bad enough seeing my own untoned body without viewing everyone else's.

However, the disappointment over the lack of a private change room was erased by the arrival of a large metal bucket containing ice and beer. After sampling the bucket, my spirits were mysteriously elevated. I pulled on my John Fluevog brogues with something approaching glee.

Out of the corner of my eye, I spied TV news anchor Hudson Mack looking natty in a black-and-tan Operations shirt. James McKenzie, CEO of Monk Office Supply, cut an awfully appealing figure in his black wool peacoat from Sand. And golly, wasn't that David Alexander of Zero One Design in a to-die-for blue flannel check Drykorn shirt, a black double-breasted Nanibon cardigan and oh-so-macho black Grenson flight boots?

Periodically, employees would pop in to ask if the beer bucket needed refreshing. The models responded with "Yes!" or "You're not kidding!" or "Beer! Beer!"

I'd imagined my catwalk stroll would be a grotesque out-of-body experience. It would be like when I was 12, making the dead-man's walk to the piano at the Nanaimo Performing Arts Festival to bang out my crude rendition of Bach, met with tepid applause.

In fact, the catwalk wasn't bad at all. Yes, there was unfortunate heckling from *Times Colonist* workmates, but bucket beers took the edge off that. And yes, Ollie the Pug did try to lick (1) everyone along the runway (2) a great big dog and (3) two little girls at the end of the catwalk. But overall it went remarkably smoothly.

Back at home, I tuned into *Say Yes to the Dress*, studying the would-be brides with renewed interest. Ollie stared glassily into the lit fireplace, no doubt reliving his fashion debut.

A DOG'S QUEST
FOR SAINTHOOD

What can we learn from a fat little pug dog?

A fair bit.

Take, for instance, the question of bravery. When it comes to being brave ... well, I'm not. Sure, I might muster up the courage to make unambiguous gestures at some faux-mohawked dolt in a Ford F-150 after he cuts me off. But that's only because I'm safely contained in my little car, equipped with a motor, wheels and—most importantly—doors that lock.

Actually, I've completely curbed my habit of doling out digital salutes following a recent encounter. As I was about to turn into our driveway, a fellow in a giant white truck jumped a stop sign, blundering into my path. I twisted my steering wheel so violently the car almost tipped.

And do you know, this guy was still chatting on a cellphone, completely oblivious to my near-death experience? This spurred me to a furious flurry of rude gestures and yells. The truck guy, a burly construction-worker type, then jumped out of his vehicle and, in a passionately delivered soliloquy, offered to give me a vigorous thrashing. I then remembered I was in an awful hurry and so continued on my merry way.

Back to the subject of bravery. Ollie, unlike me, has the

heart of a lion. Indeed, I call him Ollie the Lionhearted. Not in public, though. In public I just say "Ollie," as it's quicker and, well, makes me seem less crazy.

What's so brave about him? Well, in selecting a playmate from a group of dogs, Ollie invariably selects the biggest dog. German shepherds, Labrador retrievers, Abruzzese mastiffs, Scottish deerhounds—it's all one rich tapestry for Ollie the Pug.

We first noticed this propensity at Puppy Play School (or was it Rover Romper Room?). At the time, Ollie was a Nerf-ball-sized pup. But instead of playing with other Nerf pups, he wanted to hang with the big guys. Sometimes they'd playfully pick up Ollie in their cavernous jaws, as though checking for edibility. Then they'd gently fling him away like a discarded banana peel. Ollie just rolled over and scampered back.

"Is there something wrong with Ollie the Pug's brain?" I would wonder. "Or perhaps his doggie survival mechanism is impaired, in the manner of lemmings or those sulky teenagers who jaywalk without looking left or right."

It turns out that Ollie just likes being friendly with big dogs. I suspect he imagines that he's big, too. So it may not be a matter of bravery at all. He's just super sociable.

Indeed, Ollie is the friendliest dog I've ever known. He loves all dogs and people. On walks, he strains at his leash to make friends with everyone. Sometimes these folk are across the street. So when it's rush hour, his buddy-quest seems borderline suicidal.

It doesn't matter how peculiar or off-putting a stranger looks, Ollie wants to be his best pal. He once, for example, approached a woman dressed in what looked suspiciously like

Glad Bags. Also, this woman was in animated conversation with an invisible companion.

To my horror, Ollie bounded toward Glad Bag lady. She stopped talking, bent down and patted Ollie.

"Nice dog," she said. She smiled and walked on. A perfectly normal encounter.

Who among us cannot learn from Ollie's magnanimous, it's-all-good attitude? This dog is like Gandhi, for God's sake. Except without the spectacles and the white robe, of course.

A FEAR OF PUGS THAT GO SNORT IN THE NIGHT

By day, Ollie the Pug is mild-mannered and roly-poly. But at night, he can be incredibly frightening.

That's because he makes such peculiar noises. When he sleeps, Ollie wheezes. He moans, snorts and snuffles. He sighs and whistles like a pug-shaped calliope. The funny breathing has something to do with his pushed-in snout.

It is, in a way, endearing—like living with a little old man. Yet it's quite another matter when Ollie sneaks into our bedroom in the midnight hour for a snooze.

The other night I was in the deepest of sleeps, far into the Land of Nod. I dreamed about a dilapidated, abandoned mansion. It was grey and dark. It resembled the house from Alfred Hitchcock's *Psycho*.

It soon became apparent there was some kind of evil presence in the house. And then, this diabolical unseen thing, this wellspring of wickedness, this free-flowing fount of malfeasance, started to make a sound. It was a hoarse breathing, the sort of unholy rasp favoured by serial killers and bad guys in movies who wear hockey masks.

Convinced of my impending doom, I began to moan with fear. Of course, when you do this in your sleep, it sounds peculiar because your mouth doesn't work properly.

"Mmmmfst!" I moaned. "Mmmmfst! Mmmmfst!"

My wife sat bolt upright on her side of the bed.

"What's that noise? Is that you? What on earth are you doing? "

"Oh … God. There's someone in the room," I said groggily.

"No, there isn't."

"I'm quite certain of it. Listen."

We listened. The raspy breathing turned into a double-forte snort. I snapped on the light. Ollie the Pug blinked at us. Then, tail wagging, he tried to leap onto the bed. He was unsuccessful, as his legs are too short.

"Dammit, Ollie!" I cried. "You scared me half to death!"

Ollie wagged his tail furiously. He seemed to think we were playing a game.

For days afterward, my wife ribbed me mercilessly about this incident. She would ask if I wanted to double-check that our bedroom door was properly closed, in order to keep out our frightening dog. Whenever Ollie made a funny sound—a yowl or a yap—she would tell me not to worry, as it was only a harmless pug dog and not a murderer intent on disembowelment.

Ordinarily, I'm the first to take pleasure in teasing others. However, there was nothing humorous in these remarks. They were obviously symptomatic of some kind of defect in my wife's character—some malfunctioning humour gene—which, until now, had gone undetected by yours truly.

Last week a similar scenario occurred. Once again, it was the middle of the night. My sleep was disturbed by curious noises my wife was making. A kind of "Mmmmfst!

Mmmmfst!" Then she mumbled, "There's someone in the room!"

At this, I sat bolt upright and turned on the lights. My wife was asleep. It appeared she'd had a nightmare. And now—judging by her peaceful expression—it had passed.

Or was it a nightmare? What if there was someone in the room?

Sleep was now impossible. After a time I walked into the living room. Ollie the Pug was snoozing on the couch, snorting and wheezing.

And then it came to me.

If the murderous intruder confronted us, Ollie would surely try to make friends with him. During this distraction, I'd alert my wife to the situation. While she dealt with it, I'd lock the bedroom door and dive under the sheets.

And then I'd make that "Mmmmfst! Mmmmfst!" noise.

A GOLDEN DAY FOR CANADA
GOES TO THE DOGS

Sunday was the day of the Big Game. The most important hockey game in Canadian Olympic history. Heck, the most important event known to man, really.

It also happened to coincide with the day my wife wanted to take Ollie the Pug doggie dancing. At her request, some weeks ago, I had booked Ollie for a session. Then I forgot.

Oh, what joy I felt that Sunday morning. U.S.A. versus Canada for the gold medal! Over the fence, I noticed my neighbours had already fired up the backyard barbecue for a pre-game soirée.

"You are wise, my friends," I thought, nodding approvingly at an enormous man whose face was painted like the Canadian flag.

To be honest, I don't know much about hockey. In preparation for the Big Game, I donned my special red Olympian pyjamas. Then I organized my hockey snacks: Cheezies and beer. I was dumping the Cheezies into a bowl (and inserting one into my mouth) when my wife entered the room.

"What are you doing?" she said.

"Getting ready for the Big Game."

"Big Game? What are you talking about? We're taking Ollie doggie dancing today. It starts at noon."

"Is that today?" I asked. My jaw went slack. A half-chewed Cheezie slipped from my mouth to the floor, Ollie, sensing an opportunity, gobbled it up.

Thank God you weren't there to witness the scene that followed. For there was pleading, cajoling and begging. There was imploring and even a little beseeching. Not a pretty sight.

Surely, I suggested, there would be other days for doggie dancing! Why, Lord, oh why did doggie dancing have to occur on this day, possibly the most important of my life? Except for my wedding day, of course. And the day our daughter was born. So the third most important day, really.

"You'll be able to watch it when we get back," said my wife. "Those silly games go on for hours."

We left the house with Ollie in tow.

"Hey, where are you going?" asked my neighbour. "Big Game starts soon."

Before I could stop her, my wife replied. "We're taking Ollie doggie dancing."

Oh, there was chuckling. Not to mention guffaws, chortles and snickers. And none of it came from me.

On the way to doggie dancing, I told my wife she'd have to dance with Ollie. I couldn't picture myself prancing about, holding Ollie's front paws. It would make me feel (1) unmanly and (2) like a knob.

Doggie dancing isn't called doggie dancing. It is more correctly known as canine freestyle dancing, although most trainers just call it "freestyle." We met expert instructor Lenore Baskin, a nice woman who teaches freestyle classes at a studio in North Saanich.

Lenore was with her friends, Kathy and Kristen, who collectively form a competitive doggie dance team. Each wore a T-shirt with a dog skeleton on it. Kristen demonstrated a dance with her dog, Brody, to a pop tune entitled "Lollipop."

As the music played, Brody wove expertly between Kristen's legs, skooched backwards and did plenty of other intricate stuff. Very impressive.

Kathy, meanwhile, said that Ollie the Pug displayed the raw talent required for doggie dancing. He was already zig-zagging between her legs with tremendous zeal. Although, I think his zeal was mostly fuelled by a chunk of hotdog in her hand.

Kathy also said Ollie was smart. This was surprising, as I'd always imagined he wasn't the sharpest tool in the dog-house. For example, if you throw Ollie's stuffed rabbit across the room, he often seems absolutely gob-stopped, as though the toy has disappeared into a parallel universe.

The doggie dance team rebuked me gently when I revealed my dull-tool theory. Thinking a dog is dumb is not cool, they said. Dogs should be accepted as individuals.

After 45 minutes of enjoyable doggie dancing, I sprinted to the car and we drove home.

"Don't drive like a maniac," my wife advised.

I caught the last hour or so of the game. It was the best bit, really. Ollie the Pug sat beside me, licking Cheezie dust from my fingers.

As for my wife, well, she had an après-doggie-dancing glow to her cheeks. So it turned out to be a win-win day, after all.

ABSENCE MAKES A CANINE HEART GROW FONDER

Ollie the Pug requires a hug every single time we return home.

I don't mean after we've left the house for five minutes. It's when you're gone for an hour or more. Ollie first regards you solemnly from the front window—only his little round head is visible. Then, when you open the front door, he dashes over like Ben Johnson after a Stanozolo cocktail.

Ollie will wimper and yowl in delight, wagging his tail so vigorously the entire back portion of his body wiggles. He practically goes bonkers. The quickest and most efficient way to calm him is to hug him.

Perhaps the mechanical pressure of the embrace has a settling effect, just like Temple Grandin and her famous cattle press. It's more likely, of course, that Ollie just wants that reassuring human touch.

This is a good therapy, not only for Ollie, but yours truly. You see, I'm not a big hugger. So perhaps hugging our dog is good practice.

Hugging is a funny thing. These days, when you visit folk—relatives, friends—you're supposed to hug them. When did this all start? Heck, in the days of yore, there was precious little hugging that I can recall. You'd visit and there would be no hugs. Unless some family member had died or something. Then there'd be a perfunctory one.

At social gatherings, if you were a guy, you'd offer the other fellow a brisk, firm handshake. And then everyone would have high-balls. Now you're supposed to embrace everyone like crazy. Like we all live in a hippie commune. Like we're all Italians or something.

How did this Euro-hippie orgy of hugging come about? It's as though some powerful underground committee— some influential Emily Post-ers—had a summit meeting. At the top of the agenda: Casual Hugging—Should We or Shouldn't We?

"You know, fellas, I think we North Americans should hug more," declares the committee head. His name is Scooter or Jay-Jay; he wears a collarless shirt and a macramé vest.

It appears hugging is on the rise. For instance, the *New York Times* reported recently that frequent social hugging is all the rage in U.S. high schools. So much so that some students complain of peer pressure to hug to fit in. Some high schools even banned hugging or imposed a three-second rule.

At the George G. White School in Hillsdale, N.J., they actually banned hugging. "It was needless hugging ... it was happening all day," said principal Noreen Hajinlian (who no doubt is super fun at staff parties).

Anyway, I think hugging Ollie has relaxed me sufficiently so that, on special occasions—like Christmas or New Year's— I will hug actual people. A cross-over effect, if you will.

Ollie the Pug enjoys not only hugs but human touch of any description. He likes his belly being tickled. He likes the wrinkles in his face to be massaged. He likes his ears to be scratched.

If you do this and then stop, he'll tap you with his right paw. It means, "Hey man. Don't stop now. Continue with these highly pleasurable caresses."

This, too, has had a human overlap. The other day, I sat on the couch beside my wife. Without thinking I began to scratch behind her ear. "What are you doing?" she asked, startled.

"And aren't you a good little do … I mean, nothing," I said.

She seemed displeased. Ollie the Pug trotted over and tapped me with his paw. I flipped him over and scratched his belly.

"Hey," I said, "Check out this action."

"Don't even think about it," said my wife.

ALL HAIL CESAR

And so it came to pass that Cesar Millan, the mysterious Dog Whisperer from America, was to make a public appearance at Bosley's pet store in Victoria.

Oh, glad tidings! Forget Lourdes. Never mind about Camino de Santiago. Ollie the Pug and I would undertake a pilgrimage to meet the King of the Canines, the Prince of the Pups, the Lord of the Dance ... no, I mean, Lord of the Dogs.

On Monday, the day of the visitation, the heavens did open—in near record-setting quantities. I peered out the window, just in case Noah and his ark were navigating Marigold Road.

"You're not going to take Ollie out in that terrible downpour, are you?" said my wife.

"Oh, ye of little faith," I replied. "Can you not see Ollie and I are undertaking a pilgrimage—a crusade of almost Biblical proportions? Do not attempt to dissuade us, for your protestations shall be both fruitless and mildly irritating."

"Don't be silly. Make Ollie wear his raincoat then. And you'd better wear one, too."

"No problem."

And so I inserted Ollie the Pug into his brilliantly hued scarlet raincoat, even though it is now way too small and makes him look like a Wal-Mart-sized, Yuletide-themed sausage. The two apostles then jumped into the car and drove to Bosley's.

And lo and behold, it transpired a crowd of 200 fellow pilgrims had lined up in the rain to meet He Who Speaks to the Four-Legged Ones.

Our collective mood was giddy. After a few minutes, a woman from Bosley's popped out with an announcement: We'd have just 20 seconds apiece with the great man. A hush descended. Would it be enough?

I had hoped to solicit advice—a blessing of sorts—from Cesar. The problem? When I emerge from the shower, Ollie always licks my wet legs. Affection? Do my legs exude essential minerals lacking from his diet? Surely Cesar would know.

The Dog Whisperer's appearance was slated to run from 11:30 a.m. to 1:00 p.m. But at 11:40 a.m., the line had moved nary an inch. What did this mean?

Mostly it meant getting very wet. It poured and poured. Bosley's employees did distribute free blue plastic ponchos. Meanwhile, Ollie stood stiffly in his rain jacket, looking miserable.

My shower-mates represented a colourful cultural mosaic. There was, for instance, a middle-aged woman in a denim John Fogerty tour jacket. Another pilgrim clutched a large umbrella decorated with images of puppies and kittens embracing affectionately. The woman in front of me, in a lime-green hoodie, identified herself as "the Pet Fairy" and handed me her card.

Somewhere in the lineup, a damp dog howled mournfully. As a rivulet of rain ran down my neck, I felt like seconding the emotion.

Then came more news. We were told some fanatical Millan disciples had arrived at 10 o'clock the night before, camping out in order to be first in line. I felt the muscles in my rain-refreshed neck tense.

And then a smiling woman with a reddish-brown coon hound walked past us in the lineup. She had already had her audience with Cesar and bore glad tidings. "He's a very nice man, a nice man," she said. We all nodded—it was pretty much as we'd hoped.

The couple behind me had driven down from Duncan. The man regarded Ollie doubtfully, then related an anecdote about a friend who had also owned a pug. The dog had died of a heart attack at the tender age of two.

"Pffft," said the Duncanite, making an enthusiastic death gesture with his hand. "Just keeled over."

Disturbing. I switched my gaze to the Bosley's lady, who had returned to deliver yet another announcement: "He's signing as fast as he can! He's a very nice man!"

The time was 12:40 p.m. I'd now been waiting 85 minutes. The rain pelted mercilessly. Line-wise, some progress was made. We were now in an alley—festooned with abandoned Tim Hortons cups—beside the Bosley's building. PA speakers, covered in rain-proof garbage bags, blasted "Bad to the Bone" by George Thorogood.

And then some bad news. Very bad, in fact. The Bosley's lady, now looking harried, said, "You may or may not get in. But you will all get signed photos."

What the hey? Up and down the line there was a dark rumble of dissent. After all, we had spent more than 90 minutes in a B.C. monsoon.

At this point we had reached the back entrance of Bosley's. A black ribbon prevented our entry into the warehouse, however. The Pet Fairy suggested a small rebellion—why not boldly shove our way in? But being Canadians, we waited obediently in the downpour. Finally, we were allowed into a concrete-and-drywall holding-pen.

Yet more news from the Bosley's lady. She now said we definitely wouldn't get to meet Cesar. It was almost 1:00 p.m.—time for his leave-taking—and TV crews wanted to interview him.

There was, believe me, no joy in the holding pen. Hell hath no fury like a dog-owner scorned. People grumbled; hounds howled. Still, we hung on, just in case. Please, we thought. Oh God, please.

And then—praise be—they let another 10 people in to see Cesar. And I was number eight. Oh the joy of it! The Bosley's lady said we'd have just five seconds with him, instead of the promised 20. But there was no limit to our excruciating pleasure at being amongst the chosen ones.

Cesar Millan turned out to be a petite, rather tired-looking man in a turquoise T-shirt.

"Buenas tardes," he said politely, signing a glossy photo of himself and handing it over.

"Gracias," I said softly.

There was, alas, no time to quiz Cesar Millan about Ollie's debilitating leg-licking addiction. And yet, trudging back to my car with Ollie yanking me along, clutching my now rain-splattered relic, a feeling of elation arose from within.

Our pilgrimage had been a success. And by golly, I had whispered to the Dog Whisperer.

CLOTHES MAKE THE PUG

My wife keeps buying Ollie the Pug clothes. It's embarrassing.

Before dog ownership, I looked down on people who dressed their chihuahuas in tutus or made their English bulldogs wear Union Jack sweaters. Surely, these are the same folk who carefully arrange their antique teddy bear collections on the bed and knit multi-coloured tea cozies as Christmas gifts.

Now, my wife has become one of those who buy clothing for their dogs.

First, she bought him a much-too-small argyle sweater. It is green and white. When Ollie was inserted into it, he looked like a fashionable sausage. Or Winston Churchill poised to make a ski-hill run. After a week or two it didn't even fit at all, because Ollie had eaten too many bacon-flavoured dog snacks.

Then she bought him a little collar that makes it look like he's wearing a black bow tie.

"It's for when Ollie wants to get dressed up," she said. "Or when friends come over."

As she spoke, Ollie scampered about in a crazed fashion, trying to bite off his bow-tie collar. He seemed unappreciative of his new formal look.

She also bought him a raincoat made from a silver

synthetic material. It has a high collar. When Ollie wears it, he looks like an extra from Star Trek.

"What's up with the space dog suit?" I asked.

"It will keep him warm and dry," she said.

Ollie scampered about in a crazed fashion, trying to bite off his Star Trek outfit.

Other items purchased for Ollie: a rubber bone, two balls (one attached to a rope), a rawhide bone, a squeaky rabbit, a stuffed beagle (which Ollie likes to hump) and a stuffed squirrel. He is barely able to squeeze into his dog bed because of all this stuff.

The dog-clothes-buying binge came to a head when we visited San Miguel, Mexico. There is a shop there that sells dog clothes exclusively.

Inside, my wife spied a frog outfit. "Oh, how cute," she exclaimed. The Mexican woman behind the counter smiled sagely, saying nothing. I took this smile to mean: "Oh, you Canadian gringos. Go ahead. Buy my silly dog-frog outfit. And I will laugh, but not out loud. Only in my head. Ha!"

There was were also elephant costumes, pig costumes, cat costumes and a devil costume. I confess the El Diablo outfit appealed to me. Sadly, it was too small. For Ollie, I mean.

My wife finally settled on a tiny dog sombrero for Ollie the Pug. It is black felt, decorated with gold-coloured trim, red and green flowers and the whimsical motto: "Mexico." Tasteful? Oh my lord, yes.

When we returned to Victoria, my wife outfitted Ollie with his new hat. It has a chin-strap to prevent it falling off. Ollie scampered about in a crazed fashion, trying to bite off his sombrero.

"Aw," said my wife. " He likes it."

Can that antique teddy bear collection be far behind? Ay, caramba.

AWKWARD MOMENTS

Pets ought to come with a warning to prospective owners. The warning could be in the form of a tag attached to the pet's tail.

Such a tag might read: "Warning: Owning this animal may lead to situations you may find socially awkward and/or embarrassing."

Case in point:

The other day I was in a shopping centre parking lot. My wife had gone to the drugstore. I'm sitting in the Volvo station wagon with Ollie the Pug.

To pass the time, I amuse myself by holding Ollie on my lap and placing his paws on the steering wheel. I pretend he's driving in heavy traffic.

Just as I'm shaking Ollie's right paw as though it's a clenched fist (he's telling off an imaginary delinquent motorist) there's a sharp rap on the window.

It's our plumber. An enormous man in denim overalls who fixed our toilet last week.

"Hey there," he says. "What are you doing?"

"Nothing, really," I say.

"Playing with your doggie, it looks like."

"Yes. I mean, no. Just, you know ... doing his exercises. He has very stiff joints."

"Ah. Ha ha," says our plumber. And he walks off.

You might say I was the architect of my own social distress. In that case, yes. But sometimes, my wife is the source of Ollie-related embarrassment.

For instance, she used to dress Ollie in a too-tight argyle sweater. It made him look like an chubby comic-book character from the 1950s (perhaps "Pughead," an anthropomorphic pal of Archie and Jughead). As well, she bought him a cheesy mini-sombrero in Mexico (come to think of it, all mini-sombreros are, by definition, cheesy). On special occasions, she makes Ollie wear a collar and bowtie.

Worst of all, she bought him a bumble bee costume. It is actually a Halloween costume for toddlers she discovered at London Drugs.

I cannot over-emphasize how insane Ollie the Pug looks in this bee costume.

Last Halloween, she took him trick-or-treating wearing it. Ollie was wearing the bee costume, I mean—not my wife. Horribly embarrassing. I pray she doesn't bring it out this year.

Oddly, my wife finds nothing socially discomfiting about dressing up Ollie in nutty outfits. But she was well and truly mortified on a different, non-costumed occasion.

One night she took him on a walk. In mid-stroll, Ollie relieved himself on a neighbour's lawn.

Being a good citizen, my wife nipped over to retrieve his offering, waste bag in hand.

At that very moment, the homeowner and her young daughter pulled into the driveway.

My wife, not quite knowing what to say, said, "Oh, hello. It's quite hard to see in the dark."

Without a word, the mother slammed the car door and hurried her child into the house. Obviously, she had failed to fully grasp the situation.

My wife and Ollie made a hasty exit, lest the woman phone the police to report a female voyeur lurking on her front lawn.

"She probably thought I was a weirdo," said my wife, telling me the story afterward.

I assured her this would not be the case. But secretly, I thought—with cruel glee—yes, it must have seemed pretty darned weird, all right.

Perhaps this was some karmic or cosmic comeuppance. You know, payback for dressing Ollie up as a Mexican or a bee.

BLESSED BE THE ELEPHANTS, GIRAFFES AND PUGS

Guess what? Ollie the Pug is blessed.

I'm not just being all touchy feely or new agey. He really is blessed. You see, earlier this month, Ollie received the "blessing of the animals" at our neighbourhood church.

Here's what happened. My wife left one Saturday afternoon to take Ollie on his walk. When she returned, she was all elated and giddy-like.

"Guess what?" she said breathlessly.

"What?" I was reading the comic strip, Pearls Before Swine. It is the best comic in the world. Therefore, I do not like to be interrupted.

"Ollie is blessed," she said.

"Yes," I said. "He gets free meals, a warm bed and an obedient manservant following him, picking up his droppings and inserting them into biodegradable plastic bags."

"No," said my wife. "What I mean is, Ollie got an official blessing at the church just up the hill. From a minister. It's totally legit."

Ollie sauntered over to his water dish and began slurping enthusiastically. He didn't appear particularly blessed. In fact, he seemed pretty much the same. Except for being thirsty and all.

I'd never heard of the Blessing of the Animals before. My family were not big churchgoers. But it's exactly as it sounds. Animals of all descriptions arrive at churches to receive their blessings.

Here is Ollie's blessing. I can quote it verbatim, only because my wife brought me a copy on a little green piece of paper:

We give thanks for your life.

As you are a blessing,

So, too, may you be blessed:

With love, goodness and compassion! Amen.

My wife and Ollie had passed by Garden City United Church exactly at animal blessing time, purely by coincidence. She noticed a dozen dogs and their owners hanging about. Because Ollie loves all dogs, my wife walked right over. Or rather, Ollie yanked her over.

The minister, who had brought her own Scotty, wore Scotty-dog earrings. People sat in chairs on the lawn outside the church. They were mostly older folk, as parishioners often are these days. They were relaxed and joking around, said my wife.

"You don't usually see a group of older people joking around so much," I said, recalling a group of elderly folk I'd once seen playing bingo. They were pretty serious, mostly because they were very intent on stamping multiple bingo cards with special bingo stamps.

Anyway, at Garden City United Church, there was a bit of a call-and-response session led by the minister, with everyone following along from their Blessing of the Animals pamphlets. There were also a few readings. One suggested we are "not to be judgmental and all that kind of stuff" when it comes to our pets, said my wife.

Another reading was about what we can learn from our pets.

I looked over at Ollie. He was chewing his new rawhide bone—the special kind dipped in chicken broth. He whimpered a little, because it had yet to become soft and gooey the way chicken-broth bones do after persistent gnawing.

"We must," I thought, "learn to be patient."

"And afterwards the minister gave the animal blessing," said my wife.

Some of the animals sat nicely. Some scurried under the chairs and got tangled with their leashes. But all the animals seemed to like it pretty well. After the blessing, each lined up to have a treat plopped into his or her waiting jaws. The dogs, I mean.

Apparently, Ollie was the sole drop-in recipient at the Blessing of the Animals.

"They said I was the only one that came along because I'd seen the sign," said my wife. "Everyone was happy to see him."

I examined the green pamphlet. One prayer certainly covered the waterfront. It included not only dogs and cats, but "lions and elephants, giraffes and cheetahs." Wow.

"Did anyone bring a cheetah?"

"Don't be silly," said my wife.

She patted Ollie the Pug's head. He had fallen asleep. A blessed slumber, there was no doubt.

CALL ME GOOD BOY AND I'LL FOLLOW YOU ANYWHERE

My wife is getting good at training Ollie the Pug. Too good, in fact.

Ollie can now roll over. He sits on command and lies down. Heck, he even plays the piano. My wife holds up a treat and says, "Ollie! Play, play!" Then Ollie gets up on his hind feet and pummels the keys with his paws. Sounds like John Cage after too many whisky sours or something.

Such doggie magic occurs because my wife is patient and persistent. She's the sort of person who, if imprisoned for a long term, would construct an elaborate model of a Spanish galleon from matchsticks discarded by her jailers.

I, on the other hand, would merely use these matchsticks to poke insects that wandered into my cell. My prison nickname would be Captain Instant Gratification. Either that or Conan the Ant Slayer.

Here's the part of the story that's unsettling. You see, I have a bad habit of leaving my clothes lying around the house. In little piles on the floor.

My wife will say, "Hey, can you pick up your clothes from the floor?" And I'll do it. But after a couple of days, I'll forget. On Valentine's Day, my wife gave me a card. On the front was a picture of discarded clothes arranged in the shape of a heart.

Admittedly, all this reflects very poorly on me. However, the other day, I did remember to pick up a stray shirt from the floor.

"Good!" said my wife, noticing. "Good boy!"

Oddly, this did make me feel good. I felt like, you know, a good boy. There was an extra spring in my step, a smile on my face, a tiger in my tank.

Leaving for work the next day, I remembered something. My socks were lying on the bedroom floor. I picked them up.

"Good!" said my wife. "Good boy!"

Then it hit me. It struck me with the force experienced by John Marcher, the sad protagonist in Henry James's story *Beast in the Jungle*, when he realizes, to his horror, that he has wasted his entire life. Wait. Here's a better analogy. It struck me as it must have struck the coach of the Canadian Olympic hockey team when he realized, in Game 1, that he had used the goalie who'd failed to grasp the important "keep-the-puck-out-of-the-net" principle.

The disturbing epiphany? My wife was using dog-training tactics to train me. I am the human version of Ollie the Pug.

The nerve. I confronted her.

"Hey, are you using dog tactics to train me to pick up my clothes?"

"Yes," she said. "I am."

"And why is that?"

"Because it works," she said.

"Well … I see," I said.

Damn. It was hard to argue with that kind of logic. My wife then showed me her new book. It is *What Shamu Taught Me About Life, Love and Marriage*. It's by Amy Sutherland, who uses animal training tactics to train her husband to find his mislaid car keys and other important items.

"How did such an evil tome find its way in our house?" I asked.

"Ordered it after hearing about it on CBC. It's great. Amy is a very sensible woman."

When my wife took Ollie for a walk, I seized the book, locked the bedroom door and began reading. It turns out Sutherland learned plenty by observing how animal trainers taught hyenas to pirouette and baboons to skateboard.

A key Sutherland principle is that animals can be diverted from bad behaviour by being sidetracked. So that's why my wife presented me with a stick of celery as I reached for a beer. I forgot about the beer ... and ate the celery instead.

It's trickery. Sorcery. Voodoo, almost.

On the other hand, I am a "good boy." So I've got that going for me.

My wife is getting good at training Ollie the Pug. Too good, in fact.

CATS ARE COOL

While not a huge cat fan, I do admit they're way cooler than dogs.

Or at least pug dogs.

This became apparent the other day when I took Ollie the Pug out for his morning constitutional. Normally, Ollie doesn't notice other animals that much. His smell is acute, but his eyesight is on par with that of Mr. Magoo.

For some reason, though, he was able to spy a black and white cat lurking underneath a hedge.

If Ollie was in high school, he'd be one of those guys who are always super-enthusiastic and friendly. A real back-slapper. Bouncy and sweaty. Always jumping on your back. Probably not someone whose algebra homework you'd want to borrow.

Ollie's music collection would be mostly MP3s by Journey, Trooper and Lady Gaga. He'd be the kind of guy who has many friends who are girls, but few girlfriends, if you catch my drift. As well, he'd be among those who favoured those unfortunate MC Hammer harem-pants in the late '80s.

But this black and white cat, why, you could tell he was super cool. When Ollie dashed up to him, tongue lolling, crouching with bottom in the air (the maniacal "let's play right now!" stance), the cat scarcely batted a cat-lid.

If animals could talk, no doubt the encounter would have gone as follows:

Ollie: "Hi! Hi, hi, hi!"

Cat: "Like … hi man."

Ollie: "Ya wanna play? Wanna play? Huh?"

Cat says nothing, adjusts beret and slips on pair of Ray-Ban Wayfarers. Extracts a Gitanes ciggie from rattle-snake-skin man-bag and ignites with a silver lighter once owned by Oscar Wilde's boyfriend, Bosie.

Ollie, less certain now: "Um. OK. (Pause). Do you like eating stuff? Boy, I do. I wish I had some dried sardines!"

Cat blows French cigarette smoke in the pug dog's face. Ollie, now confused, bounces forward in an attempt to engage cat in a rousing game of Chase-Me-Charlie.

Cat: "Don't even think of it my friend. You are a pudgy little pug. Whereas I'm a cool cat. Ever heard of Herbie Mann? I've got an original 1954 copy of East Coast Jazz on the Bethlehem label. Ten-inch vinyl. Dig it."

Ollie: "Oh. Music. Do you like Lady Gaga? I do. I like to sing 'Poker Face.' You know, 'Mum mum mum mah! Mum mum mum mah!'"

Cat: "Hey. Pug boy. You have a choice. You can either leave now, you and that big oaf on the other end of your unfashionable fire-engine-red leash. Or I can claw you. Right now."

Ollie: "Wha …?"

Cat: "Don't make me cut you, man. Because I will cut you."

Me: "OK, Ollie. Let's go home now. Don't you want to play with your toy?"

Ollie: "I'm going to go home now. We're going to play with my toy."

Cat: "Whatever."

Ollie: "It's a stuffed squirrel. Licking it for hours on end gives me indescribable pleasure."

Cat: "Get out of my sight."

Ollie: " Maybe we can play later. Bye-bye!"

At home, Ollie licks his toy squirrel with gusto. For comfort, I change into the MC Hammer pants I've had since the late '80s. My wife tells me they are revolting and should be thrown out.

I chuckle, slap her on the back, hum a few bars from "3 Dressed up as a 9," and say: "Honey, you just don't know fashion."

CELEBRATING OUR NATION

The Labour Day weekend—regarded by most Canadians as summer's last joyous hoot before the back-to-school season—has once again come and gone.

This, for some reason, got me feeling sentimental about statutory holidays. For instance I recall, with great fondness, last Canada Day.

In particular, I remember taking Ollie the Pug for a Canada Day walk. This entailed taking him up and down a street in our neighbourhood.

My wife chose this particular street because a lot of residents put out Canadian flags on their lawns each Canada Day. In fact, the street was once featured on the TV news as being the most patriotic in town.

Walking up and down a street just because people stick up flags seems a curious motivation to me. To be honest, I've never fully understood the concept of patriotism. It seems an artificial notion. You know, dividing the world up with lines and boundaries, declaring which bits belong to whom, telling outsiders who can come in and who can't. And then, every year, you have a day celebrating your little bit of the Earth—telling each other you're proud to live on your little bit and so on.

I like the one-world concept—with folks helping each other out globally. At least, I like it in theory.

But my wife, upon hearing my ideas, told me I was being a curmudgeon on Canada Day.

"I want to count the flags on Agnes Street," she said. And so off we went.

In honour of Canada Day, Ollie wore a slightly insane-looking harlequin's collar. It's red and white. My wife counted the flags. Then we continued walking into a community garden. It's one of those places where different people from the neighbourhood have their own little plots.

Ollie seemed more invigorated by the community garden than the sight of Canadian flags on Agnes Street. He dashed around, sniffing everything. I plucked a couple of raspberries from a bush.

"Don't do that," said my wife.

"It's OK," I said, stuffing the berries into my mouth. "It fits in with my no boundaries, one-world concept."

As we walked home, I told my wife a story related to me by a bus-driver friend. She had once driven a route on Canada Day. In honour of the day, the bus was full of drunken celebrants. One over-refreshed rider became physically ill, leaving copious evidence of this sloshing up and down the bus's floor. Our bus-driver friend announced to the passengers that they had two options. They could drive to the depot to collect a fresh, clean bus—then continue on their way. Or they could proceed in the befouled bus.

The passengers all cried "Let's keep on going!" This, to me, seems to capture the true essence of the Canadian spirit.

"What a disgusting story," said my wife.

Ollie bounced along the sidewalk in his kooky harlequin outfit. And I, now feeling oddly cheerful, began to whistle *O Canada*.

CHOLERIC GAZE
AWAKENS GUILT

Ollie the Pug is making me feel guilty. And it's all because of his face.

We were out walking him the other day, when a little girl of four or five said, "Mummy, why is that dog so sad?"

"Oh," replied the mom, "that's just the way those pug dogs look. It's because their faces are all wrinkly. He looks worried. But he's really happy."

Ollie does have a melancholy-looking face. It reminds me of that famous Karsh photograph of Winston Churchill. When Ollie looks at me, as he does every time I make a sound louder than 10dB, his expression seems to say: "Ah, my hapless manservant, you personify the folly of all mankind. You both amuse and—to some extent—depress me."

I call it the Gaze.

Of course, just like the four-year-old's mother, I know logically that Ollie the Pug is not deliberately giving me the evil eye. Still, the Gaze always makes me feel guilty. Especially in the following situations:

a. I'm watching that engrossing reality show about cheerful, hard-working dwarves while eating a Häagen-Dazs triple-fudge-brownie-overload ice cream.

Ollie the Pug gives me a look that says: "Jeez. Just look at you. For the love of Mike. Try doing something constructive with your life. Write a novel, for God's sake."

b. Drinking a beer and reading Facebook, I respond to a person who says, "Hey, I'm thinking about making a cup of tea!" by writing, "Hey, I'm thinking about having a beer … in fact, I'm already there!"

Ollie the Pug gives me a look that says: "Jeez. Just look at you. Why not take a healthful jog instead of contributing to that unattractive spare tire, for God's sake?"

c. I'm driving when some guy cuts me off, missing my front bumper by centimetres. Annoyed, I nip in front and cut him off. Ha! Victory is mine.

Ollie the Pug gives me a look that says: "Jeez. Just look at you. Cutting off some poor sap in the manner of a testosterone-fuelled 16-year-old who's just received his learner's licence. Why don't you drive like a normal human being, for God's sake?"

Recently, the tables were turned. About a week ago, Ollie—to his huge delight—discovered a discarded chicken bone on the boulevard near our house. Each time we'd take him for a walk there, he'd sniff around, unearth this horrible bone and try to devour it.

And every time, we'd tell him to cut it out, as chicken bones can break into dangerous splinters. Besides, it's disgusting to eat mouldy chicken bones.

Last Saturday we once again passed the boulevard. Ollie, employing his powers of super-sensitive smelling, found the bone. As he stood there, chicken bone in mouth, I gave it to him. The Gaze. We stood staring at each other.

It was an old-fashioned, Clint Eastwood-style standoff. And then, by golly, Ollie dropped the bone.

My victory was short-lived. The next day I did some gardening. I trimmed some shrubs and, rather pleased with the effect, trimmed them some more. And some more.

It occurred to me that I'd created an awful gaping hole in our shrubbery. Now feeling uneasy, I turned around, only to meet Ollie the Pug's eye. He was giving me … you know … the Gaze.

"Jeez. Just look at you," he seemed to say. "When your wife comes home she'll see how you ruined the garden. And then you will be in deep, deep trouble. Now go find me a nice chicken bone, for God's sake."

CITY DOG,
COUNTRY REALITIES

Ollie the Pug is pretty much a pampered city dog. This became disappointingly apparent during our Gulf Island vacation.

On Gabriola Island, where I grew up, our family owned a black cocker spaniel named Sally. A rough 'n' tumble country dog, she'd roll merrily on dead fish and rotting seaweed. She chased sheep, despite farmers' threats to shoot on sight. And we'd regularly remove ticks embedded underneath her matted fur.

Sally enjoyed riding the Gabriola ferry. By herself. This happened after I'd left home for college. My mum told me Sally would trot three kilometres to the ferry and travel by boat to Nanaimo. She wouldn't disembark. She'd simply ride back to the island and walk home.

"How do you know this for sure?" I asked.

"The ferry men told me," said my mum.

Unfortunately, Ollie the Pug lacks Sally's rough-hewn, seafaring spirit. As we walked along the beach during our vacation, he'd carefully avoid beds of seaweed. That's because Ollie dislikes the feel of it. We also had to bypass beach areas with an over-abundance of barnacles, lest Ollie damage his delicate paws, more accustomed to prancing along city sidewalks.

Speaking of paws, my wife files Ollie's nails every day. I'm not kidding. She also brushes his teeth with special dog toothpaste.

"You shouldn't pamper Ollie so much," I told her. "He's becoming a big, coddled baby. Nothing like our dog, Sally, who regularly rode the Gabriola ferry and ran around, festooned in ticks, trying to elude the deadly aim of the farmer's rifle."

"Ollie's not a baby. He likes getting his nails filed," said my wife. "Besides, I see you giving him those 10-minute stomach rubs."

The only trait Ollie shares with Sally is a love of putrefied things. Ollie especially enjoys rolling on dead fish. Every time you looked, he'd be rolling on another one, moaning happily and waving his legs in the air. Unfortunately, his lack of country-dog smarts led to eating them as well. Ditto for washed-up jellyfish. And I'm pretty sure he gobbled some Canada geese droppings.

I awoke one morning in our holiday cabin to discover that Ollie, no doubt made ill by his deceased fish repast, had vomited in his bed. As I sat down on a couch cushion to ponder my next move (i.e., asking my wife to remove the spew) I felt something damp seep through my pajama bottoms. More dog vomit.

"What are you doing?" asked my wife, watching me twist around to inspect my pajama bottoms.

"Enjoying my vacation," I said.

A man and his dog were staying at the cabin next door.

Mango is a simply enormous yellow Labrador. The man would periodically hurl a ball into the sea. "Fetch, Mango, fetch!" he would shout. And—despite his poncy name—

Mango would catapult himself into the waves in a muy macho manner.

Ollie avoided the sea absolutely. He dislikes getting wet, you see. When it's time for his walk and it's raining, he just stands on the porch, like a furry Buddha, refusing to budge.

On the island he'd peer into tidal pools to watch crabs. That was about it.

More evidence of Ollie's lack of rustic fortitude: Every time we went into an island store, he'd cry. Even if one of us stayed in the car with Ollie, he'd still weep bitterly, pining for the lost member of his herd. To calm him, I'd croon tunes from the American songbook.

He seemed especially taken with "The Man That Got Away."

Yes, Ollie is a city dog, thoroughly pampered and spoiled. I blame my wife.

CURIOUS TALE
OF THE TONGUE

Soon after we acquired Ollie the Pug, he developed a funny habit. His tongue pokes out on one side.

I was surprised, as I thought dogs did this only in 1950s comic books. The curious thing is, Ollie's tongue is almost always sticking out.

It's pretty cute. Sometimes he looks bemused—as though reacting to the sheer absurdity of doggie existence. Other times, he looks like an amiable half-wit. It reminds me of poor Lennie in *Of Mice and Men*. Or Jessica Simpson.

Occasionally, while we're regarding Ollie during his rare tongue-in moments, he'll suddenly pop it out. Pop! It's like a tiny Whack-a-Mole. My wife and I now pop out our tongues when something weird and/or disturbing happens.

People often ask, "Why does Ollie's tongue stick out?" Having absolutely no idea, and becoming tired of saying so, I'm tempted to reply (in my best Karen Carpenter voice): "Why do birds suddenly appear every time you are near?" You see, I do not know about the tongue thing, not being a veterinarian or a canine scientist. I am simply Ollie's obedient manservant, devoted to feeding him, taking him for walks and flinging his stuffed rabbit about the living room for him to chase.

I've seen other pugs with overly long tongues. Usually, though, their tongues emerge only when they're too hot. Pugs become overheated easily, perhaps due to their squished-in snouts. But Ollie the Pug's tongue is out 90 per cent of the time. Even when he's asleep. This nocturnal protuberance becomes dry, with the unforgettable texture of a warm pencil eraser.

Perhaps Ollie's sticking-out tongue is a genetic defect. After all, he already has one. A genetic defect, I mean. Sixteen of his adult teeth failed to come in. That's a lot. It makes chewing on hard things a tricky proposition. That's why—on vet's orders—we moisten his dog pellets with warm water. I look forward to toothless old age, when my handlers will do the same for me.

It's a funny thing with animals. People feel it's perfectly acceptable to comment on their appearance in a way one would never do with humans. Why does Ollie's tongue stick out? What impertinence! Why is your bottom so enormous, madam? Why do you exhibit such a ghastly clothing sense, sir? Yes, I mean you, in the stupid Hawaiian shirt.

Not so long ago, my wife and I took a stroll down Government Street with Ollie the Pug. It seemed a good idea. Of course, I'd forgotten how Ollie will fastidiously sniff and/or lick each passerby. Progress was torturously slow.

Two women stopped to pet Ollie. One said, "Hi, Mr. Crooked Face."

At first I thought she was talking about me. But she meant Ollie. His face is kind of crooked. Asymmetrical. The wrinkles on one side do not correspond to the wrinkles on the other. Plus one of his bottom teeth sticks out. And he's a touch wall-eyed. Just a touch.

Sometimes I hardly know what eye to focus on when offering him a Tender T-Bonz Snak.

"Don't worry boy," I whispered after the women left, no doubt on a mission to purchase generously cut cargo shorts. "I got a look at those gals. They wouldn't win any beauty contest, either. And get a load of those sensible shoes."

Happily, beauty is in the eye of the beholder. Recently, I posted a picture of Ollie the Pug on a website called the Pug Village Forum. Basically, it's a site on which pug owners mostly say how cute each other's pug dog is.

Ollie's picture portrayed him in a Mexican sombrero. To be frank, he looked like a goof. Not surprising. Hat-wear is flattering to very few dogs.

Nonetheless, one of the Pug Village Forum folk responded warmly to his photo with this comment: "What a handsome boy!" Man, that made me feel like a million bucks. Take that, Mrs. Crooked Face. I stick out my lopsided tongue at ye.

DANCE LIKE YOU AREN'T AWARE OTHER PEOPLE THINK YOU'RE INSANE

Recently, my wife took our pug dog, Ollie, for a walk. During this stroll, a helpful woman stopped to inform her that Ollie is far too fat and should undertake a regime of long, healthful walks in order to lose weight.

She also said we were using the wrong kind of leash.

I was deeply saddened not to have witnessed this meeting. I'm always most appreciative when people dispense unsolicited advice on how to better manage one's lot in life.

That said, I suspect this woman missed what's truly important about our dog. Couldn't see the forest for the chub, so to speak. Little does she realize that Ollie is, despite his Pillsbury Doughboy physique, a bottomless well of philosophical wisdom.

If ever unsure of myself in any situation, I always think to myself: "What would Ollie do?" Or WWOD. Here are my dog's life lessons—I advise you to take heed in 2012.

1. Eating all the time is A-OK. The reason Ollie is so corpulent is because he devotes his brief waking hours entirely to either (a) eating food or (b) trying to acquire some. And he's as happy as a clam. A great big fat clam. So what I take from this is, Christmas gorging can—and

should—last all year. Forget that New Year's diet. It's better to die fat and happy than thin and miserable.

2. Be friendly to all. Our dog is friendly to all. If an intruder smashed through the front door with a Freddy Krueger mask and a bloody crowbar, Ollie would lick his face and nuzzle his pockets for dog treats. Yet, overall, his friendliness has been a boon. On the street, attractive women now speak to me, in order to pat Ollie. And walking a friendly pug makes it all right for an adult stranger to talk to adorable children—indeed, there's almost no danger of being apprehended by frightened parents or the authorities.

3. Take your time. Each morning, Ollie needs a short stroll around the neighbourhood in order to relieve himself. Usually, due to faulty time management, it's a rush job. I find myself saying, "Ollie, for God's sake, hurry up!" about 30 times while Ollie sniffs a putrefying leaf or nudges a discarded Slurpee container.

Does he hurry? No, he does not. The moral is, if there is a job to be done, choose exactly the right moment. And do it at your leisure. Especially when it concerns a bodily function.

4. Stick out your tongue. Due to a debilitating congenital deformity, Ollie the Pug's tongue sticks out 90 per cent of the time. It hangs to one side like a deflated piece of bubblegum, giving him the look of Curly from the Three Stooges immediately after Moe smacks him for saying "Nyuck, nyuck, nyuck!" incorrectly.

Does Ollie's unfortunate appearance impede his life pursuits (i.e. sleeping, with brief interludes of eating)? No, it does not. Therefore, my advice is don't worry overly how the world perceives you. Deep down, you are beautiful and a child of the universe. So food-stained sweatpants are A-OK, as are bulging fanny packs and that *Super Troopers* T-shirt.

5. Dance like you aren't aware people think you are insane. Every so often, Ollie does something particularly common to pug dogs. He'll indulge in what's known as a "pug run." This means, when sufficiently excited, the Ollie runs around in circles like a maniac.

It is true that phrases such as "high IQ" or "sharpest tool in the shed" or "what a smart dog" aren't ordinarily associated with this kind of behaviour. Still, it's obviously fun for Ollie. He doesn't care that he looks like a nitwit.

And neither should you. As long as you aren't breaking any laws and/or annoying anyone (particularly me), fill your boots.

There's more wisdom to be gleaned. Ollie also sheds pounds of fur, eats disgusting bones on the couch and ripped into everyone's stocking on Christmas Day.

I'm unsure of the deeper meanings here, but when I figure it out, I'll certainly pass it along to you, dear reader. In the meantime, remember: WWOD.

DOG WALK INSPIRES
HARE-BRAINED IDEA

The severity of the rabbit population explosion at the University of Victoria truly hit me last weekend.

The event raised funds for a good cause, the Capital City Volunteers, who help out old folk by driving them to the doctor and such.

The deal was, I was to give a little speech to get everyone in a giddy dog-walking mood. Then everyone would walk their dogs around the ring road at UVic.

There are many good, public-spirited people in the world. Unfortunately, I'm not one of them. And so, on the morning of the walk, I complained bitterly about having to deliver a speech.

"God. I hate giving speeches. Why do people feel the need to parade about making speeches? In my opinion, a world without speeches would be a much better world," I told my wife.

During this heartfelt monologue, I poked my fork half-heartedly into an omelette. This was a special Father's Day breakfast. However, due to late-night carousing the previous evening, the prospect of consuming eggs had lost its usual allure. My wife ending up giving most of the omelette to Ollie the Pug, who devoured it delightedly. Afterwards, in preparation for the UVic dog walk, we took him in the backyard to relieve himself.

My pre-dog-walk speech went OK—although the crowd did not seem particularly enthralled by it. And then it was time for the main event.

Guess what? If you're a pug dog, eggs can act as a potent laxative. As we ambled along Ring Road, Ollie felt the urge to move his bowels repeatedly and powerfully, despite having previously gone. Meanwhile, his habit of dashing in and out of bushes every few minutes had the effect of flushing out rabbits. Every time Ollie nipped into the shrubbery, half a dozen frightened bunnies nipped out. I've never seen so many in my life. Ollie was like the Pied Piper in reverse, only with rabbits instead of rats.

The sight of these creatures leaping out of bushes deeply excited the other dogs on the dog walk. One, a Jack Russell named Teddy, became so inflamed he yanked free from his owner to give chase. Teddy sprinted on his wee legs at terrifying speed, his leash trailing merrily behind him as his owner yelled, "Teddy! Come back, come back!" She finally caught her dog before he reached his prey.

Watching Teddy zooming along like a stealth missile gave me an idea. To solve its dire rabbit problem, UVic ought to invite all Jack Russell owners living in the Pacific Northwest to engage in a giant purge. Hundreds of these speedy terriers, bred for fox hunting, would no doubt round up these long-eared rodents in a jiffy. It would be terrific exercise for the hounds, not to mention being highly entertaining for owners and gathered spectators. It could even be a weekly event. UVic could sell beer and hot dogs to the crowd, thus raising thousands of dollars for Jack Russell Rabbit Purge Student Scholarships.

I presented this modest proposal to my wife as we strolled along Ring Road. She seemed less enthusiastic than I was, perhaps because she was so busy bagging Ollie's deposits.

As we walked past the student residences, it brought to mind the happy days of my youth. During my first year at UVic, I lived in one of these very residences. During one lively party, my mattress caught fire. This happened partly because I was introduced to a custom common to all university residences, that is, drinking cans of beer.

My mattress—damaged beyond repair—was subsequently tossed in the courtyard. The next day my parents, who were visiting, wondered aloud what a partially burned mattress was doing in the courtyard. I said I could not imagine, but speculated it was a cheeky gag hatched by college wags.

My wife, alas, seemed unable to appreciate these fond remembrances, as she was still busy with Ollie's frequent forays into the shrubbery.

Finally, we reached the end of the dog walk. We dog-walkers congratulated one another. And everyone got into their cars and drove home.

"That was a good dog walk," I said on the way.

"Truly unforgettable," said my wife.

Ollie, meanwhile, was now chewing on a squeaky rubber chicken. As my wife seemed less than talkative, I started to compose a letter in my head. It went something like this: "Dear Dean. You know that rabbit problem? Well, I have a brilliant solution …."

ON A CHICKEN WING
AND A PRAYER

My New Year's resolution is: don't feed Ollie the Pug chicken bones.

There are, apparently, many things one should not feed dogs. Who knew? Onions, for example. Nuts, chocolate, bread dough and grapes. Coffee and alcohol. Practically any food or drink that makes life enjoyable is taboo. Hence the saying, "It's a dog's life … because they can't drink espressos."

On Christmas Day, all Victoria-based Chamberlains congregated for the Big Feed. Its chief components were the Big Turkey (requiring six hours of roasting) and the Little Christmas Pudding (which, thanks to the accidental pouring of a half-bottle of brandy, led to the Big Blaze).

Assembling such a feast is a full day's work. Upon offering assistance, my wife suggested I might help by avoiding the kitchen, so as to be out of her way.

"And," she added, "don't give Ollie any chicken bones."

This was a reference to Thanksgiving of 2008—a catastrophic date within the annals of Chamberlain history. On that afternoon, after elaborate preparations, my wife and I sat on the couch to drink a glass of wine. I put on Willie Nelson's *Stardust* album. And then the power went out.

"Oh no," we both said.

"Arf," said Ollie the Pug.

Dinner was to be at 7 p.m. The food was still cooking, although now at an ever-diminishing rate. At 6 p.m., the guests arrived. The house was dark. Everyone commiserated. We lit candles. After a while, my wife—looking unhappy—suggested we order takeout.

"No, no," said the guests. "We don't mind waiting. Come sit. Relax."

In order to achieve full relaxation, some of us began to drink scotch and sodas. Then, after 20 minutes went by, I phoned up a Chinese restaurant and ordered the food.

Naturally, 10 minutes later, the lights went on.

"Yay!" exclaimed everyone, raising their glasses.

I phoned the restaurant back. The fellow there graciously cancelled the order.

By now my brother, refreshed by scotch, was amusing himself by letting Ollie the Pug lick a chicken wing (my mother brought them as hors d'oeuvres).

Ollie loved this. So I let him lick my chicken bone. Only this time he lunged up and swallowed the whole thing. A two-inch bone. I stuck my fingers in Ollie's mouth. Too late.

I felt awfully guilty. It seemed swallowing such an object, for a wee dog, would be like a human ingesting a zucchini-sized bone. That night we watched Ollie like hawks, on the look-out for signs of intestinal distress. But he seemed quite happy.

The next day I phoned the veterinarian.

"What happens if a pug dog swallows a chicken bone?" I asked.

"Look here, I'm fed up with these prank calls," he said.

"No. I'm serious."

"Well, it's not a good idea," said the vet. "Never let that happen."

The doctor declared it a waiting game. Make sure your dog is moving his bowels without distress, he advised. And sift through each and every dog excretion for chicken-bone evidence.

"So…," I said, hanging up the phone. "Who's up for chicken-bone duty?"

"You are," said my wife.

Nothing ever emerged, as far as I could tell. Perhaps powerful stomach acids caused the bone to disintegrate. Ollie seemed as cheery as ever, and has remained so.

The only tangible result from the Thanksgiving Chicken Bone Catastrophe of '08 was that I ended up tossing out the table fork employed for chicken-bone sifting. Actually, there were two tangible results. I resolved in 2009 to avoid feeding Ollie chicken bones. And it has remained on my New Year's resolution list ever since.

My wife, helpfully, has supplied me with an resolution addendum, which includes being more polite to telephone solicitors.

But one thing at a time, I say.

FISHY TREAT RAISES A STINK IN THE WRONG CROWD

While walking downtown the other day I had a brilliant idea. Why not buy some stinky fish?

That's what our family calls the tiny dried sardines you can buy in Chinatown. Our neighbour tipped me on this. Her dogs love them. You can buy an enormous bag for five bucks.

Ollie the Pug enjoys anything with a strong smell. And he's crazy about anything remotely edible. So a highly odiferous food like stinky fish is, for him, the equivalent of crack cocaine.

Here's an example of how dried sardines changed his life. Ollie hates to go outside if it's raining. He'll just sit on the porch, staring at you incredulously. But if you toss a stinky fish on the sidewalk, why, he dashes out.

Sadly, as with anything truly wonderful in life, there's a catch. If you're a human being, the smell of these dried sardines is absolutely horrific. It's ammonia-like, practically toxic. So I keep them in a hermetically sealed Tupperware container. And you can still smell them from a metre away.

Recently, I experienced an unfortunate incident related to dried sardines.

It happened at a rock concert I reviewed at the Royal

Theatre. Thirty minutes into the show, a bad smell wafted up. A vile vapour. An ungodly pong. The odour was familiar, yet unfamiliar at the same time.

"Someone has forgotten to use their deodorant," I decided.

This instantly annoyed me. If I were a politician, I'd enact a law forcing every citizen to apply under-arm deodorant each morning.

It is a contentious subject. Opinions are widely divided on the subject of underarm deodorant. Some folk believe they do not need it. Indeed, they snort contemptuously at the notion, decrying it as a legacy of the repressive 1950s. They'll lecture you on the dangers of aluminum contained in deodorants. Some will suggest the dust from crushed crystals is a preferable substitute. Say no to "the man," they say. Say no to deodorant.

These people are wrong.

So anyway, at the rock concert, I glanced over at a great big guy with a pony-tail next to me. He wore the type of shirt that, in less enlightened days, was called a "wife-beater." He held his beefy arms up high as he clapped. He was oblivious to those around him, as he was grooving hard to the sounds of Jefferson Starship. I became even more irritated. Bad enough to be at a Jefferson Starship concert without having the president of the anti-deodorant brigade moving vigorously next to you.

So I gave him a meaningful look. It was meant to convey the following message: "Could you please put down your arms." Unfortunately, he was the kind of rock concert fan who fails to notice meaningful looks. In other words, the typical rock concert fan. So I gave him another look.

And, finally, he noticed.

"Hey man," he said, pausing in mid-clap. "What's your problem?"

Suddenly, like magic, my attitude changed. I flashed to a memory of getting pummelled by some meaty teen in high school. Turned out to be an amateur boxer.

"Sorry?" I said. "Problem?"

"Yeah," he said. Then he sniffed the air.

"Hey, what's the smell? Is that you?"

What? The nerve of this guy. Talk about impertinence. I inhaled.

And then it struck me like a lightning bolt—with the force of Leonardo da Vinci conceiving the *Mona Lisa* or Stephen Harper deciding singing Beatles songs in public is a really good idea. I still had Ollie's dried sardines in my jacket pocket. Gingerly, as the pony-tailed one watched, I fondled the bag in my pocket. The top was open.

"Ah, you're smelling my dog's treats."

"What?" he said.

"Sardines, sardines!" I yelled into his ear. "Here, in my treat bag!"

He seemed not to comprehend me. So I pulled out the bag. Of course, a silvery shower of tiny dried sardines spilled out. The big guy gazed at me in amazement, even though Jefferson Starship was at that very minute launching into "White Rabbit."

All of this has taught me a valuable life lesson. Never, ever carry a bag of dried sardines on your person. Me? I've switched over to the Snausages Party Snack.

FRINGING AND RETCHING

Pets never get sick at convenient times. Still, I wish Ollie the Pug hadn't become violently ill during the Victoria Fringe Theatre Festival.

Writing about the Fringe is the entertainment reporter's equivalent of running a marathon. One year two of us covered 64 shows.

Typically, after putting in time at the office, you attend your first show at 6 p.m. You rush from one to another until 11 p.m. You write reviews until about 12:30 a.m. And then you do it all again the next day.

This continues for a week. Plenty of sleep is essential.

My wife and I attended a Fringe show called *The Human Body Project*. Although officially work for me, this was to be our date-night for the week.

Twelve of us gathered in a tiny art studio. We sat in a semi-circle, which—in my experience—is invariably a precursor of bad things to come.

A middle-age woman in glasses wandered in. She was naked. No one said a word, including her.

What's the correct etiquette when a naked person enters a room? Does one look at the naked person? Does one avert one's eyes? Do you say to your companion, "Hey, get a load of that?"

After a long and awkward silence, the nudist, a.k.a. Tasha Diamant, said, "I think you all knew you were going to see a naked lady, right?"

Yes, we all said. Except for my wife.

"I didn't know this was going to be a naked-lady show," she whispered.

"Oh yes, I'm pretty sure I mentioned it," I whispered back.

Tasha then told us she required a few minutes of silence to "feel the room." She said she would close her eyes during this process of room-feeling so we could absorb her nakedness without inhibition.

It was an odd show. No script. Just her chatting with the audience—and plenty of awkward silences. It was like a new-age therapy session one might encounter at a Gulf Island resort. You know, "Discovering Your Inner Nudist in a Non-Rolfing Context." That sort of thing.

My wife was less than overjoyed by our evening at the theatre. I continued to attend Fringe shows that night—alone.

Later at home, writing my reviews, I noticed Ollie the Pug was agitated. Instead of snoring as is his midnight custom, he pranced about crazily.

"Cut it out Ollie," I said. "Cut out that crazy prancing."

He dashed upstairs and ran around like a maniac. Then he came down to tear around the living room some more.

I finally got to bed at 1 a.m. Three hours later, something was scratching the bedroom door and crying. It was Ollie.

"I'll get it," said my wife.

At 7 a.m., I woke up. My wife was wearily pulling the cover from a couch cushion.

"Ollie vomited all over the love seat," she said. He had also been sick in his bed. He'd urinated in the basement. And, as a sort of doggie pièce de résistance or magnum opus, Ollie had defecated on the futon.

Normally this would be cause for reprimand. But Ollie was clearly not himself. He was lethargic. He had bumps all over his body. A web search suggested mange or ringworm. We booked a Sunday veterinary appointment.

Saturday was another gruelling night of Fringing. Four shows in a row. One was *The Big Smoke*, in which a sensitive young man struggles to accept his emerging homosexuality. During one key scene (climactic both figuratively and literally) I started to feel terribly itchy.

"Oh God no," I thought. "Ringworm. Or possibly the mange."

That night I experienced horrific mange dreams. Sleep was interrupted by the urge to scratch. And then, at 3 a.m., another wake-up call: Ollie was retching again.

Fortunately, the next day the vet said Ollie had merely experienced an allergic reaction to something he had gobbled on the road. He had two shots and was immediately back to normal.

For this week's date night I suggested the Fringe again. "Hey, how about *Misadventures of a Massage Therapist*?"

"No," said my wife.

"*Psycho Bitch*?"

"That had better be the name of a play," said my wife.

"It is," I said.

"No," she said

Some folk just don't appreciate the arts.

GOOD THING IT COMES
ONLY ONCE A YEAR

Christmas can be a bewildering, even frightening time for
dogs. Or at least, it was for Ollie the Pug.

The first thing that threw him was saxophone-playing
Santa. If you switch Santa on, he plays Jingle Bells on his
saxophone and does a funny dance. Jolly old St. Nick
shakes his hips in a curiously serpentine manner that's
almost erotic, bringing to mind Dita Von Teese or Lady
Gaga. Perhaps it was made in a country where the notion of
Christmas is profoundly different.

Ollie the Pug was amazed when Santa started dancing.
He leapt this way and that to avoid the toy's strange Yuletide
boogie. He was even more aghast when it fell over. Santa
kept up his vigorous gyrations on the floor, as though
undergoing an epileptic fit. Ollie sprinted down the hall
in fright.

Just before Christmas, we drove to Nanaimo to see my
wife's sister and family. On the way, we told Ollie the Pug
he was to be reunited with his old friend, Charlie, a terrier/
poodle cross.

When Charlie spotted Ollie, we realized their friendship
had changed. Charlie became enraged by the sight of a chubby,
pig-like dog trotting about his domain. He barked and bared

his teeth in that demonic way dogs do. Friendly ol' Charlie was now Charles the Ferocious—Angry Guardian of the Gates of Hades. Ollie almost fell down in his effort to escape. It was even more frightening than saxophone-playing Santa.

It was decided the two must be kept separate. First, Charlie was banished to the laundry room. Then it was Ollie's turn. If Ollie went near the laundry room during Charlie's timeout, Charlie would detect his presence and bark like mad. No doubt he was making his demon face at the same time.

Finally, it was time for bed. It was decreed that, in the interest of keeping the peace, Ollie the Pug would sleep in our bedroom. I had reservations about this. Ollie's pushed-in snout makes the act of breathing a loud and laborious exercise. But my wife assured me everything would be just peachy.

You know how sounds are amplified when you're in bed at night? Passing cars, creaky boards, the knock of baseboard heaters? Try sharing the room with Ollie the Pug. I kept having dreams in which Maurice Sendak-like monsters gasped and moaned as they chased me in and out of caves.

Just for laughs, Ollie would occasionally wake and jump up on my side of the bed. You know, just to see what I was up to. Mostly, I was trying to get back to that Maurice Sendak dream. What Ollie really wanted to do was climb onto the bed. But his legs are too short for successful bed ascension. And he's too portly. So instead, I kept getting these regular wake-up calls.

On Christmas Day, back in Victoria, we were worried Ollie might disrupt Christmas as my sister's dog, Rosie, had.

When she and her family were briefly gone from the house, Rosie tore her way into all the gifts. Happily, Ollie seemed uninterested in the packages under the tree. He was keen on Christmas decorations made of gingerbread, though. He climbed on the arm of the couch and was poised to fling himself into the tree for a clandestine chow-down. We caught him just in time.

There was one final surprise in store for Ollie. I'd given my wife bright-red pyjamas as a Christmas gift. In the store, they'd appeared to be a tasteful burgundy colour. But when my wife opened the package, the pyjamas had mysteriously turned a violent shade of vermilion. They were the colour of Remembrance Day poppies. Only much, much brighter. My wife, seeming slightly startled by her pyjamas, tried them on. When Ollie saw this brilliantly red apparition appear in front of him, he started barking violently. His reaction seemed to be: "Oh, for the love of God, what on Earth is this strange and devilish creature? Surely this horrible thing—with a skin colour not found in nature—is about to slay me!"

"Sorry your pyjamas are such a peculiar hue," I said to my wife. "Oh no, they're just fine," she said.

Ollie barked again, then dashed off to hide in the kitchen.

"Well," she said. "Did you keep the receipt?"

HAIR OF THE DOG DOESN'T MIX WITH SCOTCH

If there's one thing I hate, it's animal hairs that fail to stay attached to the body of the animal in question.

Take, for example, those cat owners who stride about with their sweaters—usually black—encrusted with cat hairs. Yuck. To me, this shows an utter disregard for personal hygiene.

Surely, those who appear in public with sweaters swathed in pet hair are also card-carrying members of that not-so-exclusive club: We Who Shower Only for Special Occasions. Not to mention that spin-off fraternity: We Who See No Real Need for Deodorant Because it Contains Dangerous Aluminum or Something.

If I were on a blind date and the date person showed up with cat hairs decorating her sweater, I'd end that date right there. "Goodbye," I'd say. "Go home and make liberal use of your lint-remover, that is, if you even own such a device."

So imagine my horror when I realized that Ollie the Pug sheds a lot of hair. Lots. Apparently, pugs are a heavy-shedding breed. Who knew? As Ollie saunters about the house with his tongue sticking out, little clouds of pug hair shoot out merrily from his pudgy body. They waft up into the air, then collect in clumps in corners of the room.

In the Adrian Chamberlain "Golden Book of All Things Disgusting" (a weighty compendium growing larger daily) this ranks as … well, pretty darned disgusting.

Ollie's hair seems to get into everything. The other day, for instance, I was going to drink some scotch from my special scotch glass. This glass is made from crystal. It has a stem. The glass tapers from the bowl, then turns out toward the rim. No one is allowed to touch the special scotch glass but me.

So anyway, I poured some scotch in my glass and sat down in my special comfy chair. I turned on my calming Philip Glass solo CD, the one in which he plays the same arpeggio for two hours. I lifted the glass to my lips and—horror of horrors—there was an Ollie hair stuck to the rim.

"Quick, quick! Come here!" I yelled.

"What's wrong?"

"There's a pug hair stuck to my glass," I said.

"Pig hair?" said my wife.

"No, pug. Pug, pug, pug."

"What? Is that all? Don't be silly. I thought it was some emergency, for goshsakes. Just pull it off."

I did so. But believe me, the scotch-drinking experience was absolutely ruined. I kept thinking about that famous surrealist sculpture by Meret Oppenheim. You know, the fur-covered cup and saucer? It was all very upsetting—although you'd never know, judging by my wife's callous attitude.

Some readers might ask, "Why not give your house a vigorous vacuum-cleaning every once in a while you lazy sod, so as to get rid of all that pug hair?"

Good point. In fact, I do. Well, not me exactly. We have a house-cleaner who comes in once a week. After she vacuums, the Chamberlain household looks as clean and hair-free as it did in the carefree days of yore. Then Ollie walks in. Ten minutes later, the rooms are as hair-clogged as ever.

"Well," you might say, "why not comb your pug dog's fur on a daily basis, you booze-swilling swine, thus ridding your premises of surplus hair?" In fact, I do. Well, not me exactly. My wife brushes Ollie most days with a special metal comb/rake thing. It's called the Furminator. It's a high-quality de-shedding device. Ollie likes it when she brushes his stomach. He makes grunting noises and peculiar faces.

But still … the hair falls out.

As a result, I've resorted to Plan B. Plan B consists of me buying lint rollers all the time. For convenience, they are cached in strategic locations throughout the house.

Before leaving the house, I seize the closest lint-brush and de-hair myself. I seem to spend half my life running a lint roller over my body.

I even have nightmares about it, in which yours truly is chased by giant lint-rollers.

After a thorough lint-rolling session, I'll be virtually dog-hair-free. But then, upon returning to the Chamberlain household (a.k.a. the "House o' Hair") it's back to Square One. Ollie dashes gleefully into my arms, wagging his tail so vigorously his entire body shakes. And once again, I am completely hair-covered.

Although it is nice to get such a warm welcome.

HE'S SMARTER THAN
YOUR AVERAGE PUG

We all think our children are smart. And it appears the same goes for our pets.

I once knew someone who owned a chihuahua so dim, it almost needed a personal assistant to escort it from one room to the next. It was terribly inbred. Fudgie reminded me of the banjo player from *Deliverance*—only he couldn't play the banjo.

Despite all, the micro-brained chihuahua's abilities were held in tremendously high regard by his owner. Any of Fudgie's behaviours, no matter how inane, were regarded as evidence of superior intellect. If the dog started biting your toe, his eyes all crazily askew, she would say, "Oh Fudgie, thanks for protecting Mommy!" Or if he was lying on a newspaper, tongue sticking out to one side, she'd say: "Oh, Fudgie, you're such a great paperweight!" (OK, that's a slight exaggeration.)

Anyway, sometimes I think Ollie the Pug is smart. Other days, well ... not so smart.

For instance, my wife has trained Ollie to play the piano. Of course, he doesn't really play. He scrambles up to the piano on his hind legs and whacks at the keys with his front paws. And that's only if you hold a sliver of freeze-dried liver in front of him. Still, in the world of dogs, it's fairly impressive stuff—perhaps the equivalent of the fellow who can recite *The Wreck of the Hesperus* by heart, or the yoga expert who wraps both legs behind her head.

On the flip side, Ollie also chases his tail. He'll twist around and, to his utter amazement, notice this curled, furry thing. It will enrage him, as though some villain sneaked up behind him—perhaps in his sleep—and glued an unsuitable appendage to his body.

Ollie will growl, then give chase. He is never quite able to capture his fuzzy nemesis. Does that discourage him? No.

Tail-chasing always seems to me proof-positive of a low doggie IQ. It's like when you meet someone new at a party. The person seems likable, attractive, intelligent. And then he or she pulls a "tail-chaser," that is, says something that lowers your estimation of their intellect.

It might be: "Boy, you know, I really enjoy reading the *Family Circus* comic strip." Or "My favourite singer? Definitely Céline Dion." Or "Gosh, I just read *Twilight* by Stephenie Meyer. And hands-down, she is the greatest author ever." Or "I don't know much about art, but I just adore all those painted eagle statues in downtown Victoria."

Why not cut through the chit-chat and simply a wear a sign that says, "My brain is the size of a pumpkin seed"?

Perhaps I'm being too harsh. There may be Céline Dion fans who hold PhDs in microbiology. And I freely confess to doing all kinds of stupid things myself, such as tuning in to *Dancing With the Stars* or watching the movie *Super Troopers* repeatedly.

Nonetheless, the tail-chasing caper got me wondering as to how bright Ollie really is.

With this in mind, I found a website with a dog IQ test. The test must be scientifically valid, because it was created by "pet expert" Warren Eckstein of *The Today Show*.

For the first experiment we put a blanket on Ollie's head. Top score if the dog escapes in 15 seconds. Fifteen seconds went by. Then 30. No movement.

"Oh man," I said. "Is he asleep?"

Ollie did much better on the other tests, though. For another one, you show your dog a treat, then stick it under one of three buckets. You then turn your dog so he's facing the other way. After that, if he goes to the treat bucket, he passes. Ollie passed.

We tallied up his score at the end. Ollie the Pug did quite well. He's no Lassie. But he's no Fudgie, either.

My wife then noticed an IQ test for human beings on the computer.

"Hey, I've got an idea," she said. "Why don't you take an IQ test, too?"

"That's OK," I said. "I think I have the kind of intelligence not easily tested. You know. Emotional intelligence. Or intuitive intelligence. I forget which."

My wife's Mona Lisa expression was difficult to read. Ditto for Ollie the Pug. For he'd now fallen asleep, his tongue lolling to one side.

LESSONS FROM
A TONGUE-LOLLING PUG

There are many wise sages to learn from: Plato, Gandhi, Nelson Mandela. Not to mention Bono, Wayne Dyer and Jon Stewart.

I would add Ollie the Pug to that list. Believe it or not, many important life lessons can be learned from a fat pug dog whose tongue lolls out crazily and who is missing 16 adult teeth.

For instance:

Television is not reality: Ollie occasionally glances at the TV, usually when dogs bark. But he seems not to "see" what's happening. Comprehension appears to be zilch.

It reminds me of a story about primitive African people. These culturally isolated tribesmen could not comprehend a smiley-face drawing of a face. It was because they were unfamiliar with the symbolism: That a bowed line represents a smile, and so on.

Anyway, Ollie's seeming gormlessness might actually be wisdom. After all, television is not reality. Ollie is merely rejecting a somnambulistic, techno-driven aspect of our culture.

On the flip side, our poor dog is missing some excellent programming. Like *Glee* ... and that other one where midgets drive tractors.

Dogged persistence pays off: We've instructed our dog

not to chew rawhide bones on the couch about 1,347 times. But every once in a while, Ollie vaults to the couch with his gooey bone, attempting to get in a clandestine chaw. It might be minutes before anyone notices that Ollie has, once again, achieved this plateau of double happiness (comfy couch, nauseating bone).

He reminds me of those nightclub Don Juans who hit on every girl. Sure, they fail 999 times out of 1,000. But that one-thousandth time equals pay dirt. Admirable, no?

Be afraid ... be very afraid: Many curious things terrify Ollie. When we carved our Halloween pumpkins (or rather, I ate a Blizzard while my wife carved them), Ollie took one look at these jagged-toothed visages and fled in pure fright.

Ollie has also been scared by a folding table, a recycling bin, a lawn ornament and a flowerpot. This might seem silly. But in fact, it is stone-cold wisdom. Play it safe, says Ollie, and nothing untoward will happen.

Amen. Heck, I'm not going to answer the door anymore. Ditto for the phone.

Know when to throw your weight around: Back to Halloween. A small girl of about two or three came to our door dressed as a butterfly. Ollie (perhaps realizing she wasn't a flowerpot or a folding table) leapt on the child in a bouncy, friendly fashion.

The girl promptly flopped backwards into the large wicker basket we use for mail delivery. Her father laughed. All-round hilarity ensued. As haiku master Masaoka Shiki once wrote: "There are few things more joyous in life than witnessing a startled toddler being tipped by a family pet into a sturdy household receptacle."

Go with the flow: Ollie the Pug is a tremendously placid dog. This trait allows you to pose him in any fashion, and he'll retain the pose.

I often prop him upright in a humanoid sitting position, leaning back, so he looks like a furry old man with a pot belly. Pop a rawhide stick into his mouth and viola: Winston Churchill. I've whiled away many a rainy afternoon in this fashion; it's tremendously amusing.

The moral? Ignore those fears about looking foolish. Just relax, for gosh sakes.

Don't be afraid to ask: When he wants someone to scratch his stomach or massage his incredibly wrinkled face, Ollie will often do a curious thing. He'll tap you on the leg with his paw.

He does it all the time. He taps. You scratch. It can go on for hours.

Surely, we humans can use such calmly assertive behaviour as a model. Don't be timid; speak up to your partner. Tap, tap—can I have a massage? No? Well—tap, tap, tap—how about a gin rickey? No? Well—tap, tap, tap, tap—can you drive over to Dairy Queen and buy me a Blizzard which, in turn, will augment my pleasure as I watch this episode of *Glee*?

I haven't tried this. But let me know how it works out for you.

NEUTERING AND
OTHER DELIGHTS

Imagine if your doctor deemed it necessary to remove your testicles.

You'd be sitting in his (or her) office, making small talk about your prostate gland and the like. And then he (or she) would say, "By the way, it's really time to get the old testicles cut off. Snip, snip. Say … I've got an opening Tuesday."

But the doc's last words would be lost. That's because you'd be half-way down the hall, sprinting as furiously as possible with one hand protecting the nether regions.

Recently, the news came down for Ollie the Pug. Our vet decreed it was time for neutering. Upon arriving home, I regarded Ollie sadly.

"Bad news, old chum," I said. "Tough luck."

Ollie pulled out his rawhide bone and, as is his custom, solemnly placed it on my shoe and commenced chewing vigorously.

Weeks ago, my wife had promised to go to a concert with me. But when that turned out to be N-Day, she declined.

"I must stay here, at home, with Ollie," she said.

"Why, what's up?"

"He's getting neutered. If you were getting neutered, I'd stay at home with you," she said.

"Ah, yes … the neutering," I said. "No need to explain or speculate further."

When Ollie the Pug arrived home from the vet that fateful afternoon, he was not a happy camper. He seemed all groggy. And his tail—usually coiled joyfully—was straight as a chop-stick. Not only that, Ollie's habit of sticking his tongue out had caused it to completely dry out. His tongue felt like a pencil eraser again. Apparently, he lacked the strength or the will to pull it back in. Poor little guy.

I went to the concert. No choice, as I was reviewing for the newspaper. When I returned around 11:30 p.m., everyone was in bed. Ollie was awake, though. Apparently, hours of drug-induced slumber had refreshed him tremendously. As I closed the front door he capered about excitedly.

"Shush," I whispered as he tried to bite my toes. "Go to sleep, Ollie. You've had a tough day, buddy."

What a surprising turn of events. Gosh, if someone removed my testicles, I'd curl and remain quiet for a long, long time. Like a decade. Ollie's attitude was quite different.

He even started to do his pug run around the house. He'd reached such a state of ecstatic joyousness, the only recourse was dashing about in circles like a madman.

It was now almost midnight.

"God, Ollie," I said. "Cool your boots. Everyone's trying to sleep. No pug run. No pug run!"

Ollie went into a cheeky bowing stance (front legs laid flat, head up, bottom wiggling in air) that means: "Come, let us have fun and merrily caper about."

"No Ollie," I said. "No capering after midnight. You might pull out your stitches."

If I had any sleeping pills or Quaaludes, I would have popped one on his tongue—now sticking out but thoroughly wet.

The hall light switched on. It was my wife in her dressing gown.

"What are you doing with Ollie?" she said. "He seems really animated."

She looked at Ollie, who jumped up and licked her ear.

"Nothing, I swear. Guess he's back to normal more or less. Only, you know … more rested than usual."

I led Ollie back to his pen, then closed the room's door. He began to whimper, but I think this was less about residual neutering pain and more about not being taken for walkies.

The next morning, Ollie still seemed OK. His stitches looked fine. But later on my wife was concerned. He hadn't had a bowel movement all day.

"Don't worry," I said. "He's off his schedule, what with his testicles being removed and all. He'll probably have a good BM tomorrow."

My wife looked concerned and unconvinced.

"And I bet it will be a really big one, too," I said, trying to cheer her up.

And by golly, you know what? He did. And it was.

NOBODY EXPECTED
THE PUG INQUISITION

A friend of ours just purchased a pug dog. The process was spectacularly daunting.

She acquired the dog through a non-local breeder. With this particular outfit, one must fill out a questionnaire. This intimidating form rivals the Spanish Inquisition-style grilling a social worker might direct at a couple hoping to adopt a child. Especially if the couple were crack dealers or something.

Sample questions:

- Will you be willing to spend $500 a year minimum on your puppy?
- Are you willing to send me copies of your vet reports for important matters?
- Are you planning on moving in the next year?
- How much do you anticipate spending yearly to feed, vaccinate and provide medical care for your pet?
- What types of supplies do you have (or plan to get) for your pug?

The questionnaire requires details on your family, including the ages of children. You must state whether everyone is in favour of pug adoption—and if not, you explain this sad state of affairs. You must say how many hours a day your pug will be left alone, and exactly where it will be kept when alone. (It does not ask how the solitary confinement room is decorated, although I'm sure this weighed heavily on the inquisitor's mind.)

And finally: Are you willing to take responsibility for this pug for the rest of its life?

Golly. I'm glad we didn't face all of this with Ollie the Pug. I'd surely have cracked under the pressure and provided inappropriate answers, thus derailing the transaction.

The unexpectedness of "Are you willing to take responsibility for this pug for the rest of its life?" might have thrown me. No doubt I'd have blown it in the manner of Sir Galahad in *Monty Python and the Holy Grail.*

Bridgekeeper: "What is your favourite colour?"

Galahad: "Blue. No, yel …" (Sound of screaming as Galahad is hurled over a cliff.)

True story: As you might recall, when we first met Ollie the Pug's breeders, I accidentally dropped one of the pups when it squirmed unexpectedly in my hands. The hapless pug dropped a foot onto the hardwood floor, making a theatrical "bonk!" sound. Fortunately it was OK. And no one seemed to mind, really.

But the questionnaire-from-Hades folk, presented with such a heinous gaffe, would doubtlessly have frog-marched me to the door. They'd have heaved me to the sidewalk with profanities and a side-order of violent kicks to the bottom.

And then I'd be arrested or something.

Our friend did plenty of reading before entering the hallowed hall of pug dog ownership. We did, too. It's a good idea, as pugs are a distinctive breed not suited to all.

Here are a few tips:

Expect mega-shedding: Imagine an animal that puffs out explosions of fur every time it breathes. Imagine—at least in the case of fawn pugs—never being able to wear the colour black again (take heed, Catholic nuns!). Imagine encountering battalions of "dust bunnies" in all nooks and crannies. Only these bunnies are constructed from pug hair rather than lint.

House-training: I'd always believed pups could be house-trained in a week or two. When I was a kid, we trained our cocker spaniel immediately. And it was a fantastically dumb animal.

Pugs are notoriously difficult to house-train. They have pea-sized bladders. Beyond that, they're incredibly stubborn. If a pug figures your new Turkish rug is a nice, comfortable berth for its offerings, it's tough to convince him otherwise. It took an entire year for Ollie the Pug to be weaned from my Turkish rug. Luckily, the rug has a very intricate pattern.

Me and my shadow: If you do not enjoy the singular sensation of being followed from room to room, do not buy a pug. Like all pugs, Ollie tracks me like a diligent and furry KGB agent. From the biggest room in the house to the smallest room, if you catch my drift. And he's intensely curious about everything you do. Imagine being licked, rolled on and gnawed by a pug during all house-bound activities. And I do mean all.

But hey … aside from that, it's all good.

OH MANSERVANT,
I'VE VOMITED AGAIN

First there was Facebook. And now there's Twitter, a tremendous advance for mankind.

With Facebook, we're able to send valuable information to friends and acquaintances about how our days are going. You know, stuff like, "Now I'm thinking of getting a cup of tea," followed by "Still pondering that cup o' tea ... boiling water is such a chore! LOL," and "Gone off the whole tea idea. CTN, TTFN, ROFL."

Twitter, as we all know, is a micro-blogging service. We use it to send each other micro-messages called tweets. This is a huge advantage over Facebook, although exactly what that advantage is escapes me at the moment.

This got me thinking—what if our pets could Twitter? Or tweet. Here's what Ollie the Pug's tweets would be like:

8 a.m. Man, I'm going to sleep in again today. I'm terribly fatigued. If I wasn't a pug dog with paws instead of hands, I'd place cucumber slices on my eyes.

8:12 a.m. What was that? Sounds like a knife on a cutting board. Is someone preparing food?

8:13 a.m. Is someone preparing food?

8:14 a.m. Is someone preparing food? OMG. This is just insane!

8:15 a.m. Nah. It was just my manservant, Adrian. He dropped his deodorant stick. Sure sounded like a knife on a cutting board, though.

8:22 a.m. Just had breakfast. Tasty. Wish there was more grub, though. Hey … what's this on the floor? Dirt? Food? Dirt? Food? I'll eat it.

8:31 a.m. My manservant doesn't seem to mind cleaning up my vomit.

8:40 a.m. Guess what? I'm outside. My manservant keeps saying "potty!" But I'm just not into defecation at the moment. Hey, a dried-up spider. Yum.

8:55 a.m. My manservant doesn't seem to mind cleaning up my vomit.

5:15 p.m. Man, that was some power nap. Had that strange Lassie dream again. You know, the one where Lassie's wearing an enormous cat mask? Rather Fellini-esque. Shouldn't have eaten that spider, I guess.

5:16 p.m. Is that someone pulling up in the driveway?

5:17 p.m. OMG, I really think that's someone pulling up in the driveway!

5:18 p.m. It's my manservant. I feel the urge to caper about joyfully, making peculiar strangulated noises.

7:34 p.m. I'm going on my walkies now. Not so much walking … I mostly sniff stuff. If I see a dried-up dead bird, I devour it. Hey … there's one.

7:56 p.m. My manservant doesn't seem to mind cleaning up my vomit.

8:17 p.m. I've got my toy squirrel in my mouth. Chase me, for the love of God! Chase me, chase me … zzzz. Zzzz. Zzzz.

OLLIE AND THE BEAN BAG

Now that Ollie the Pug has undergone the operation that strikes fear into the hearts of all men—not to mention dogs—he has all but abandoned one of his favourite pastimes.

That would be (forgive the crudity) humping. Nowadays, he'll occasionally mount his favourite toy—a life-sized rabbit. But the old gusto has more or less vanished. Ollie attempts to get friendly with Mr. Rabbit in a lackadaisical, almost absent-minded manner. It reminds me of the pipe-smoking octogenarian who, upon gazing at a pretty girl, is reminded of his vigorous but distant youth.

It's a far cry from the days of yore, when Ollie mounted everything with maniacal glee. Back then, the chief object of his affections was a toy dog. The toy contains a bean bag. It's really meant for humans, not dogs. You're supposed to heat up the bean bag in the microwave, insert it into the toy dog, then apply it to your sore neck. But we never used it much, as the bean bag smelled peculiar after microwaving.

Anyway, in his bacchanalian, pre-neutered days, Ollie the Pug loved the bean-bag dog. He'd clutch it with his paws and pivot like a jackhammer. It was disconcerting. You see, I still viewed Ollie as a baby. And babies don't usually do that kind of thing.

I think it was my wife who first noticed our dog's new

hobby. "Ollie's starting to express his carnal nature," she said one day.

"Excuse me?"

"Yes," she said.

God, no. Not cute little Ollie.

Later that morning, sitting at the computer in my dressing gown, I sensed an urgent vibration near my feet. What on earth could it be? A gravel truck rumbling by? A minor earthquake?

It was Ollie the Pug.

"Ollie," I said. "What do you think you're doing?"

He released the bean-bag dog and gazed up. He looked guilty.

"Bad dog. Bad dog." Yet after a moment or two, I felt bad. Ollie was only doing what comes naturally. Why, who am I to divert a pattern forged by Mother Nature over the eons?

"Um, OK," I said. "Go back to your bean-bag dog."

By this time, however, Ollie had lost interest. Perhaps his feelings were hurt. He sauntered off and started to bite the sofa. I believe in psychology, this is what they call transference.

Not long after, friends came for a visit. As we sipped cocktails, I related the tale of Ollie and his risqué exploits. I produced Exhibit A, the bean-bag dog. My friend Mike, whom I've known since high-school, examined it. He held it like a puppet, pretending to make it talk.

"Hey Ollie baby," said Mike, making the bean-bag dog wiggle its hips. "What do you say to some hoochie-koochie?

Ollie looked at the toy uncomprehendingly, then stared at Mike. Then I took the bean-bag dog.

"Ollie. Ollie. Look. Me love you long time," I said, jiggling the toy in an alluring manner.

Still, no response. Apparently, matters of the heart cannot be forced. And truth be told, I felt rather mean to be teasing Ollie like this.

The next morning, sitting at the kitchen table with my coffee, I sensed a wee tremor. In my legs. Oh God, was I having a stroke? Happily, no, it was merely vibrations emanating from Ollie and his bean-bag dog. Yes indeed, the star-crossed lovers were united once more.

This time I said nothing. For I knew Ollie's scheduled visit to the vet for a certain procedure was merely weeks away. Why not let the little tyke enjoy himself while he could?

And so, between sips of coffee and flips of newspaper pages, I began to sing, softly: "You're once, twice ... three times, a bean-bag dog."

OLLIE EATS ON EARPLUG

Ollie the Pug eats everything. Dung, dirt, paper, gum. I wonder if this is normal, or whether it signifies something is missing from his diet. Like earplugs.

One recent Saturday, I drove to the beach with Ollie. I was on a mission. You see, the municipal worker who removes our garbage every two weeks (why not every week?) had had an accident. There's a sort of a depression in our lawn, about the size of a mud puddle. He stuck his foot into it while hoisting a garbage can and twisted his ankle.

I know, because he left a note on the garbage can that said: "I twisted my ankle in your hole. Please build a proper path to your garbage cans."

Currently, there is no real path to the garbage cans. There's just, well, lawn. And that little depression. Garbage men have negotiated this treacherous terrain for about 20 years without toppling into this hole.

I phoned Saanich municipal hall. A clerk suggested that—while constructing a new path was not necessary—filling in the hole was.

So I set off to the beach to obtain stones and sand. My plan was to fill the hole, then top it with soil and grass seeds. I figured the trip would be a diversion for Ollie, so he came along.

As soon as we set out, Ollie began to go absolutely mental in the car. Maybe because it's a convertible and the top was down. The wind excited him terribly. I kept one hand on his leash so he wouldn't leap out, and with the other steered and shifted gears. It's not something I would recommend to the novice. At one point, to obtain a more desirable view, Ollie clambered onto my head.

We made it without mishap. But on the way back, Ollie discovered a pair of earplugs on the floor of the car. He started chewing them madly.

"Ollie, Ollie! No, no! Bad dog!" I yelled while reaching down and trying to pry his jaws apart. This is difficult to do while manipulating a stick shift.

At home, I found only one of the earplugs. The other was missing. Ollie had obviously swallowed it. And apparently, without any detrimental results … he seemed quite chipper.

That night I had to review a Heart concert at the arena. The tickets were good ones, in the second row. Ordinarily, this would be cause for rejoicing. But we're talking about a hard-rocking band that hasn't turned down its amps since 1976. Three painful seconds into "Kick It Out," I grabbed for my earplugs. Of course, thanks to Ollie the Pug, there was now only one.

After the show I returned home in a disoriented state. One of my ears was fine. The other felt like it had been hammered with a Louisville Slugger.

"Look," said my wife, greeting me cheerfully in the hallway. "I found your other earplug."

It was all misshapen, like a wad of chewed gum. For some inexplicable reason (perhaps confused after two hours of relentless electric guitars and drums), I shoved it into my ear.

"Yuck," said my wife. "What are you doing? Ollie coughed that up."

"What?"

"He made a funny, throat-clearing sort of noise. Then he coughed it up."

I seized the coughed-up earplug and flung it across the living room. Ollie regarded me in an alert, interested manner.

Several days later, there was another note taped to the garbage can. It was a form note. A box beside the word "vector" was checked. And beside that, the garbage man had written: "Rats!"

Puzzling. I thought "vector" was something to do with mapping. Co-ordinates and so forth. What could rats have do with this? But my wife said vector can also mean something that transmits disease. Like rats.

The garbage man was now obviously embarking on a reign of terror. First the depression (which I'd since filled) and now rats. I examined the offending garbage can, which is rusted and has a gaping hole on the bottom. Time to buy a new one.

So I got into the Volvo. At that moment, my wife appeared on the porch with our dog. She waved and pointed to Ollie, his tail wagging maniacally, obviously wanting to ride in the car.

"Can't hear you!" I yelled. "Ear! Still ringing! Sorry!"

Ha. Victory was mine. Sort of.

OLLIE ENTERS
AGE OF CAUTION

With age comes caution. This is natural, of course—and perhaps a little sad.

Ollie the Pug is the most friendly animal I've ever known. As a puppy, he'd dash up to every living thing with slobbering affection. But after being growled at and nipped repeatedly (by dogs, not people) his approach has become considerably more wary.

Now, if Ollie spies another mutt, he bows down subserviently, bottom in the air. If the would-be friend makes any welcoming gesture (tail wag, batting an eyelid) Ollie gallops over.

If the dog fails to respond, Ollie retreats dejectedly—toddling off in the soul-crushed manner of a man who has lost his life savings in a poker game.

Oddly, our dog's caution sometimes extends to inanimate objects. Ollie gets fed twice a day. The funny thing is how warily he approaches his dish.

He always gets the same grub: kibble (special brand for chubby dogs), a dollop of yogurt and bits of meat. And every time his food is presented, Ollie partakes of an odd ritual.

Me: "Ollie! Suppertime!"

Ollie, entering the kitchen with marked air of indifference:

"Ah yes. The dinner dish. Greetings, my old nemesis. Do you think I'll easily succumb to your oh-so-seductive charms?"

Dinner dish: (No response)

Ollie, circling dish with self-conscious casualness: "Because really, I have no interest in you ... Well, what's this? Meat? I suppose I could manage a quick peck."

And then he scarfs down his food in 23 seconds.

Why the faux hesitation? Can anyone explain this routine? This is a dog who adores food, who will eat anything: strawberries, pickles, zucchini, vitamin pills, ear plugs.

There is a formal, almost theatrical aspect to Ollie's puggie pre-dinner ceremony. It puts me in mind of Noh drama or arcane Roman Catholic ritual.

It's the same when Ollie relieves himself. Does he attend to his business promptly, as one would desire? No. Instead, he must indulge in the ritual of tootling around endlessly, finding the optimum location for his contribution.

This is especially annoying in the morning, as I hustle him down the street before setting off to work.

Me: "Ollie. Potty. Potty. Quickly."

Ollie sniffs discarded Kleenex, then rubs his muzzle for two minutes through someone's dew-laden lawn.

Me: "For goshsakes, Ollie. Just go. Stop screwing around."

Ollie rolls on his back. Notices schoolboy across the road. Attempts suicidal dash across the street to make friends, despite bumper-to-bumper traffic.

Me, yanking on leash: "Ollie. No. Just go. Go, go, go, go."

After 15 minutes, Ollie strolls in a circle—a good sign.

Sniffs pine cone. Lifts head alertly as automobile backfires. Returns to inhale the pine cone. Walks in more circles. And then, finally, he accomplishes the task that really ought to have been completed 14 1/2 minutes go.

Walking home, I notice other poor saps standing in their front yards, dejectedly holding leashes, waiting for their dogs to follow Ollie's suit. This miserable job falls to us, as our wives are too busy with important morning tasks, such as the application of makeup.

The temptation is to exchange a few words with my fellow sufferers, to commiserate. But I'm too cautious, too wary—and so say nothing.

OLLIE FANCIES
A CHICKEN DINNER

We took Ollie the Pug to the petting zoo last Sunday.

The original notion was to take him for a nice long walk—part of his stay-trim health regime. We were going to stroll along Dallas Road. Instead, we detoured to Beacon Hill Park.

Then I had a brilliant idea. Why not take Ollie to the petting zoo?

Why, he could frolic with the lambs, bunnies and alpacas. I imagined Ollie could be at one with his fellow creatures. You know, just like the animals who played in perfect harmony while waiting for Noah to build his ark.

Sometimes the animals would say, "Hey Noah, is the ark ready yet?" And Noah would say, "No, I'm having a technical problem with the rudder." And the animals would say, "No problem. Take your time, as we are quite content to play in perfect harmony." Not that the animals would understand the intricacies of rudder installation or anything.

"The petting zoo?" said my wife. "Are you nuts? I don't think they let dogs into zoos."

But apparently they do. In any case, the girl at the admission booth didn't notice our chubby pug scooting in, straining at his leash like a maniac.

First, Ollie dashed over to the chickens. He was especially interested in a noisy rooster. When the rooster crowed, Ollie shoved his face into the wire fence, staring intently. I suspect he was thinking, "I enjoy the rooster's throaty, clarion call. Plus, I'd really like to eat him."

Indeed, many of the animals at the Beacon Hill Park petting zoo are of the edible variety. There is, for example, a pig. It was asleep. Come to think of it, any pig I've ever seen outside the supermarket has been asleep.

In the non-edible category, we saw a miniature donkey and its brand-new donkey baby. This wee donkey was just a day old. It leapt about skittishly, as though testing its brand-new legs. A crowd gathered.

The public was invited to fill out a form in which one could propose a name for the donkey baby. My wife filled it out.

"What did you write down?" I asked.

"Gumby. You know, like that donkey from Gumby and Pokey," she said.

"Gumby was the little green man. And come to think of it, Pokey wasn't a donkey, he was a pony," I said.

I suggested my wife retrieve her form and correct it, but she wouldn't hear of it.

Some of the children seemed as interested in Ollie the Pug as they were in the zoo animals. One patted Ollie and said he was cute.

On the drive home, my wife said, "That was nice how the kids really liked seeing Ollie."

"Yes. I was tempted to tell them Ollie was actually a petting zoo animal who'd gotten loose. I could say he was an unusually large hamster."

"But you were able to contain yourself."

"Yes," I said.

Such commendable constraint made me feel mature, like a real adult. Ollie, meanwhile, was sound asleep and moving his jaws in a vigorous fashion. Perhaps he was dreaming of eating that rooster. Or the pig. Or both.

OLLIE IS A NATURAL
IN THE POOL

Like many of his breed, Ollie the Pug continually wages the battle of the bulge. Or rather, we do it for him, as Ollie's personal motto appears to be: "I will gobble food until I burst like a piñata."

At 25 pounds, Ollie is, apparently, one pound over the "Gosh, is your pug ever fat!" limit. So I decided to get a doggie boot-camp happening for him.

"I've decided to get a doggie boot-camp happening for Ollie the Pug," I told my wife.

"Get one happening for yourself at the same time," she replied.

What a heartless comment. It's true I gained a few pounds over Christmas. Fortunately, with my sub-endomorphic build, no one notices. Except my wife.

Anyway, you can imagine my glee upon stumbling across something called K9 Fit Fur Fun. It's a new pool exercise program for dogs that just opened in North Saanich. According to the K9 Fit Fur Fun folk, swimming improves a dog's strength and is a superior cardio and respiratory workout.

I contacted Cory Greenstein, who runs the program. He suggested Ollie the Pug try an introductory pool session. So one evening Ollie, my wife and I drove out to North Saanich.

The pool is at a private residence where various doggie courses are offered. Including dog dancing! I didn't know dogs could dance. Apparently, there's choreography involved, too.

Cory turned out to be a soft-spoken young fellow with an enormous tiger tattoo on his chest. I figured he must be a winning combination of gentleness and firmness.

The saltwater pool is impressive: 14-by-36 feet, four feet deep, heated to 28 C. I imagined I'd be swimming with Ollie as well—like those lucky souls who swim with dolphins. So I'd brought along the horribly bright green (and now too small) shorts that serve as my swimwear. Fortunately, Cory said there was no need for me to enter the pool, unless I was really keen. Which I wasn't, really.

First off, he stuffed Ollie into a green-yellow doggie life-jacket. Then Cory held him over the water. Air-borne Ollie, looking startled, immediately started moving his legs in a slow motion. I imagine it's a deep-seated canine swimming instinct. Although Cory said he coached one poodle who didn't move his legs at all. The poodle just bobbed in the water like a furry cork.

Turns out Ollie, with virtually zero experience, could swim right off the bat. Mind you, he always made a bee-line to the pool's edge. My wife and I stood on the sidelines, cheering and clapping.

I wonder what Ollie made of all this. Perhaps he thought he was being drowned, with his owners inexplicably applauding the procedure. Still, I think he enjoyed swimming on the whole.

But Ollie was not crazy about surfing. At one point,

Cory placed Ollie on a little surfboard. He stood shakily on all fours, puzzled and shivering.

K9 Fit Fur Fun offers many doggie swim programs. One is for weight loss. There's also a three-minute open swim (a come-one, come-all affair), an "introduction to water" (for the fearful novice) and athletic toning (for the cutting-edge jock-dog). There are also sessions for dogs either going into or recovering from surgery.

Pool exercise is pretty intense. As soon as we got Ollie back in the car, he promptly fell asleep.

"Wow. Look at that," I said.

"Yes," said my wife.

"Hey, maybe we should enroll Ollie in those doggie dance lessons as well. Just to kick this whole boot-camp caper into high gear."

"We can do that just as soon as you and I sign up for ballroom dance lessons," she said. I became deathly quiet. Outside, a lone cricket chirped. A plaintive, lonely sound.

The last time we took ballroom dance lessons was years ago in Castlegar. A vaguely sinister guy called Freddie led the class. Freddie always danced with one hand placed delicately on his stomach, above his waistband.

You know, I think it's probably best for Ollie if we just stick to the occasional pool session.

OLLIE MAKES THE
PERFECT B-BUDDY

We all have at least one person in our lives on whose behalf we must apologize on a regular basis.

This person is a loose cannon. This is someone who says, or does, all kinds of socially inappropriate things.

I think of these people as "barbarian buddies," or b-buddies for short. Charlie Sheen is probably the most famous example today.

No doubt he's promised friends many times he'll stop cavorting with prostitutes, snorting cocaine and saying weird stuff about tiger's blood and trolls.

And then he does it again and again.

When I was 21 and living in Nanaimo, I had a b-buddy for a roommate. Crazy Bob (not his real name) was highly intelligent and lots of fun. He also liked to drink with great gusto, then get into scrapes. He'd say peculiar things to girls we were trying to meet. He'd "borrow" your clothes and then return them covered in grass stains.

His craziest escapade was downing a bottle of Bacardi, then zooming off in his Galaxie 500. Perhaps mistaking it for the street, Crazy Bob plowed into a downtown parking meter.

The meter's pole became badly entangled in the car's radiator.

His efforts to reverse and continue his inebriated joyride were thus foiled. A passing cab driver phoned the police—he was thrown in jail.

Early the next morning, I got a phone call from Crazy Bob requesting a ride home from the police station. He told me the whole story, but—as usual—seemed unrepentant.

The Crazy Bobs in our lives tend to fade out as we get real jobs, mortgages and wives who don't approve of Crazy Bob.

However, this creates a void—a vacuum effect—which must be filled.

For a time, our daughter stepped in to take over the role. This is when she was a toddler. She wasn't smashing cars, of course. But she was spitting out food, madly flinging My Little Ponies and dashing around with no pants. She was, in short, a miniature b-buddy, a diminutive John Belushi determined to transform our home into *Animal House*.

Then she grew up. Once again, there was a b-buddy void to fill. Enter our new pug dog, Ollie—a rambunctious, slobbering, grunting maniac.

A month ago, we stayed in Vancouver for a week. We'd found an online site where one can rent suites in people's homes. My wife selected a studio basement suite because it allowed pets. For some reason, she wanted to bring Ollie.

It was working out pretty well. However, the owners of the house did something that worried me. They allowed Ollie to enter the upstairs of their home on a regular basis.

"It's OK," they said. "We simply adore dogs."

On my birthday, we had dinner at a restaurant, leaving Ollie in the fenced backyard of the house. We took the

SkyTrain back and walked the block to our rented abode. Then, because I needed to use the bathroom badly, I started to sprint ahead of the others.

On the steps I spied the owner. From his animated body language, I could see he badly wanted to talk to me.

"No time to chat!" I said cheerfully, making ambiguous hand signals while running into the basement suite. The owner buttonholed my wife a minute later.

"Your dog went upstairs into my daughter's bedroom," he said. "And he took a big dump on her eiderdown. It used to be white."

I cringed as I overheard this, holed up in the basement suite. What an unfortunate social gaffe!

What would Emily Post say? Was there even an entry in her etiquette book for this sort of thing?

We felt absolutely terrible, of course. We presented the owner with flowers, wine and money for dry-cleaning. I have a feeling their pet-friendly policy has been rescinded, however.

Driving home to Victoria the next day, Ollie snored away in the back seat. Oblivious. Happy. Completely unrepentant.

In other words, a typical b-buddy.

OLLIE MEETS HIS PUPPET
DOPPELGANGER

I am now the proud owner of an Ollie the Pug puppet. It looks just like Ollie.

Let me tell you, this puppet is a real feather in my cap. It puts a swagger in my step. After all, how many Victoria dog owners have in their possession a custom-made puppet modelled on their very own dog?

Not only that, my Ollie puppet is handcrafted by Victoria's Tim Gosley, a professional puppeteer who was once Basil Bear on the Canadian version of Sesame Street.

The road to owning an Ollie the Pug puppet was long and arduous, my friends. It goes back several months, when Theatre Inconnu asked if my soul band would play a fundraising event for them. Like most arts groups in town, Theatre Inconnu is poised to be sucker-punched by the Liberal government's cuts to gaming grants for cultural organizations.

The band agreed to play. Then Gosley, the event's organizer, suggested it be an Ollie the Pug-themed fundraiser. This didn't particularly make sense to me. I wasn't sure what our pug dog had to do with Theatre Inconnu.

Gosley explained he wanted to construct an Ollie the Pug puppet. The puppet, operated by him, would host the event. Then he'd auction it to raise money.

It seemed a quintessentially West Coast notion. No doubt in Toronto, theatre companies mount glitzy fundraising events overseen by tuxedo-clad dignitaries. But here in Victoria, we have a dance MC'ed by a pug dog puppet. Not only that, Gosley said he'd create a new-age light show to illuminate the proceedings.

Tim Gosley is a nice fellow. But once you get involved with him, it's like joining the mafia or something. You become embroiled in strange events—unorthodox happenings that, if you were thinking clearly, perhaps you'd rather not become embroiled in.

Gosley now said he needed to interrogate me, in the guise of the Ollie the Pug puppet, about arts funding in B.C. This interview would be videotaped beforehand and screened at the dance.

It sounded a bit weird.

"Don't worry," Gosley said. "I'll make sure there's no light on your face, just like those guys on TV from witness protection programs. We'll call you the Unknown Critic. No one will know who you are, you see."

I wasn't sure I wanted to be the Unknown Critic or be interviewed by a dog puppet. But my wife told me to be a good sport and go along with it.

In his basement Gosley set up the equipment and lowered the lights. Then, waggling the Ollie the Pug puppet and speaking in a crazy-sounding puppet voice, he quizzed me on arts funding in B.C.

Being interviewed by a pug dog puppet in a darkened room is a singular experience. As the puppet grilled me, I experienced a sort of out-of-body feeling, as though I'd ingested a mysterious psychedelic drug. Could this really be happening?

After a couple of hours, it was all over. Then, returning home, I found a new e-mail from Gosley. Somehow, his computer had lost our interview. Could we do it all again?

"Oh my God!" I yelled.

"What?" said my wife.

I ranted and raved. Bad enough being interviewed by a pug dog puppet once. There was no way I could do it again. But my wife reminded me it was a good cause. So we did it all over again—after which I had an enormous martini.

Gosley wanted the real Ollie to make an appearance at the event, now entitled Theatre Inconnu's Summer Blowout with Ollie the Pug Puppet. So my wife brought our dog along, outfitting him in a harlequin clown collar that made him look slightly demented.

At the dance, Gosley invited the real Ollie on stage, then, with a flourish, produced the puppet. Real Ollie stared at his doppelgänger in absolute amazement. When Gosley started talking in that funny voice, Ollie barked fiercely at his new nemesis. I experienced that psychedelic drug feeling again.

As the evening wound down, there were just a few silent bids on the Ollie puppet.

"You'd better bid," said my wife.

"I don't want a dog puppet," I said. "Plus the bidding's gone up to $100."

She reminded me that is was good cause. And so, at the last minute, I placed a $110 bid. And yes, victory was mine.

Gosley still has the puppet. He's now modifying it or something. When I showed Ollie the Pug a photograph of it, he barked and growled. No doubt oodles of dog puppet fun awaits us all.

OLLIE THE WATCHDOG

I wish Ollie the Pug was a better watchdog. What a comfort that would be.

When it comes to watchdog duties, Ollie's greatest handicap is size. He weighs 25 pounds. That's good for a pug. But not so good when a hulking intruder with a crowbar is lurching about in your hallway.

Ollie is roughly the shape and size of a small pig. In fact, my wife's nickname for him is "Pig." But a real pig would be far more helpful in the watchdog department. For one thing, pigs are capable of desperate acts of feral aggression, as I once discovered at the Saanich Fair.

Boy, if I were a burglar encountering a pig during a break-in, I'd make like Donovan Bailey at the 1996 Olympics. And there's an added bonus—a sort of subtext— to owning a watch-pig. Burglars will think, "Hey, if this guy owns a pig, who knows what other dangerous animals are in the house? Like maybe a super-crazy chimp."

Another disqualification for Ollie's watchdog career is his super-affability. If he sees anyone, he'll try to run over and make friends. This makes walking Ollie a challenge, as he's always straining to cross traffic-clogged streets to greet passing pedestrians.

If a stranger knocks on our door he'll bark once or twice.

But these barks are small and yelpy. And they're merely a prelude to Ollie running over—tail and bottom wagging furiously—to lick the hand of any potential Jeffrey Dahmer plotting to murder yours truly.

If I seem overly concerned about home invasions, it's because a burglar once slipped into our house at night through faulty French doors. He stole my wallet and my wife's purse as we slept.

Afterwards, I purchased a Louisville Slugger and kept it under the bed. This seemed a good idea until my wife pointed out that if I tried wielding my Louisville Slugger, the intruder would simply seize it and commence pummelling me.

I've also obtained, via illicit means, a small canister of mace. My wife tells me that, in the event of a break-in, I'll likely spray myself in the eyes, thus rendering myself temporarily blind. Still, it makes me feel better, having that mace. Not to mention the Louisville Slugger.

We also have an alarm system, which routinely sends false alarms, bringing exasperated policemen to our door. Before that, I tried to save money by buying a mail-order gizmo. It is, essentially, an electronic speaker that's supposed to make loud barking sounds to ward off intruders. The picture on the box shows a masked villain fleeing from a ferocious Doberman pinscher. This image gladdened my heart.

"What's that?" my wife said when it arrived.

"Dog alarm. You know, for burglars."

"Ha," she said.

"Check out the picture on the box. Just you watch."

When I tried it, one could indeed hear a Doberman pinscher barking. However, it sounded as if it was several miles away. Maybe in a neighbouring town. Not only that, the soft barking was fuzzy and scratchy. It sounded like the very first primitive recordings, the ones predating Edison's phonograph, but not as loud.

I phoned the company that sold me the gizmo. It took 20 minutes to get through. "This thing won't scare away intruders. It's not loud enough," I told the receptionist.

"Check the box," she said. "It says, 'For amusement purposes only.' "

"Amusement? But what about intruders?"

"For your amusement only," she said. "Have a good day and enjoy your barking dog box."

So I've decided to work one-on-one with Ollie to improve his bark. My method is as follows: I bark, and then Ollie gets a liver treat if he follows suit. Then I start barking louder and louder, with him duplicating the feat.

So far it has just been me barking, with Ollie the Pug gazing at me blankly, wondering why I don't hand over the stupid liver treat. But I just figure it's a matter of time.

OLLIE'S OWNER IS MADE
IN THE SHADES
— IF THEY FIT

The other day, my daughter and her friend had their pictures taken with Ollie the Pug.

They are a photogenic young couple. Ollie, on the other hand, is not so photogenic.

For starters, in each photo the flash had turned his eyes a demonic white-blue. As well, being in my daughter's arms pushed up all his saggy neck skin, making him rather unattractive. It looked like Ollie the Pug melted in the sun or something. Plus, as usual, his tongue was lolling out in a manner that suggested a deranged Elizabethan peasant.

"He looks like a big, fat mess," said my daughter, vowing to display only Ollie-free images from this series.

Ah, poor Ollie. I know how he feels, suffering from a similar problem. Although generally pleased upon looking in the mirror ("Why … hello Brad Pitt!"), for some reason, I find photographs of me always depict an impostor with a pumpkin-like head and a red face. It must be some trick of the camera.

Anyway, as we studied the demon-eyed photos of Ollie, a bold idea came to me. I placed a pair of my sunglasses on Ollie's face. In this way, he could avoid debilitating retinal reflection. Plus, wearing shades, he sort of looked like a dog version of Horatio Caine from *CSI: Miami*.

But the plan failed. Ollie shrugged off the glasses and glared. They clattered to the ground. Ollie started to chew them. No problem. You see, I've got about half a dozen pairs. That's because some guy keeps sending me sunglasses in the mail.

Here's the story. Recently, I lost my sunglasses on an airplane. This was distressing, as it's hard for me to find sunglasses to fit my large head. Drugstore sunglasses are too small—it feels like a plastic vise has gripped my cranium.

I found an online advertisement for "XL big-fit sunglasses." Great. But when they arrived, they were too small. Naturally, I complained. The seller offered to send me another pair for free. These, he promised, would truly be XL. But they were exactly like the first pair. Once again, it felt as if a small but powerful monkey was applying acupressure to my skull.

I complained again. Yet another pair arrived. And then, for some reason, another. They were all the same. It was very curious.

"Why do all these sunglasses keep arriving in the mail?" asked my wife.

"I can't say, exactly," I said. "But they're all on the small side."

It was time to get serious. Some other guy on eBay advertised sunglasses with this tantalizing description: "Jumbo-head sunglasses fit large heads." And, if this wasn't enough, these words appeared over an image of a smiling watermelon.

There was also a photograph of a big-headed U.S. postman wearing them. "Our mail carrier loves his jumbo-head sunglasses," the caption said. "The bigger your head, the better the fit!"

This seemed right up my alley. So I ordered a pair. They've yet to arrive, but I have high hopes. It's not as if I'm hydrocephalic or anything. But sometimes, at the theatre, people sitting behind me complain about my head obstructing their view.

Of course, none of this helps Ollie the Pug in the home-photography department. Maybe we just need to position him in a more flattering manner. Perhaps he can adopt a model-like stance, like those women who pose with their feet in that becoming Audrey-Hepburn-esque manner. Or those who stand at an angle, in order to appear less wide. I must look into this.

ONE DOESN'T SIMPLY
ANOINT ONESELF TOP DOG

Ever hear of the alpha dog concept? I hadn't, at least, not until we got Ollie the Pug.

The theory is that dogs believe their human families aren't people, but rather, packs of dogs. And within this dog/human pack, there is competition for the position of top dog. Or the alpha dog.

Writes one expert: "It is your responsibility to establish yourself in the alpha position. If you fail to do this, your dog will do it as a natural behaviour."

Naturally, I wanted to establish myself in the alpha dog position. The article suggested holding your pet's forepaws and staring into his eyes. If he struggles, you growl at him. So I grabbed Ollie, gazed into his eyes and growled.

He stopped squirming and cocked his head in amazement. Ollie looked like that Jack Russell from the old RCA Victor ads. His attitude seemed to say, "What up, crazy man?"

At that moment, my wife walked in.

"What are you doing with Ollie?" she asked.

I got up from my knees.

"Nothing. Well … actually I'm establishing my dominance. You know. Letting him know who's top dog in this family."

My wife laughed. This laughing went on for a long time. A length of time some would call ... unseemly.

"And since when did you become top dog in this family?" she said, wiping tears from her eyes.

She had a point. It's probably hard to believe, but in the Chamberlain household, I am not top dog. In fact, I'm quite possibly bottom dog. Although I hope and pray this is not true.

You see, my wife constantly tells me what to do. In addition, she writes out elaborate lists of tasks for me to complete each weekend. Surely, this is irrefutable evidence of top dog-dom.

It is true that I do not complete many of these assigned tasks. Some weekends, I do not complete any. Rather, I wander about the house and yard, doing random things that appeal to me. Once, instead of cleaning up the remains of a dead rat in our crawl-space, I bought a used beer fridge.

Nonetheless, the bottom line is that my wife, having achieved the dominant status of list-maker, is top dog. She is the alpha human, the honcho, el-supremo, the Schwarzenegger-ian governor of the state of Chamberlain. And, since my daughter assumes command of the TV remote, I suspect she is higher in the chain of command than me.

So you can understand my enthusiasm to establish dominance over Ollie, the new member of the family. Otherwise all would be lost.

Lately, however, even Ollie has taken to usurping my authority.

In the past, to the idle passerby, it must have appeared I

was dragging our dog rather than walking him. Ollie would stop to sniff every dandelion or grass tuft, savouring eau de doggie. He'd stop to eat anything resembling food, whether petrified gum or congealing Slurpee in a discarded paper cup.

But lately, Ollie has started dragging me around. He presses ahead powerfully, like a bulldog, wiggling his bottom purposefully. When I suggest we take a side road, he regards me disdainfully. His expression says, "Ah, the presumption that you are in charge—while tiresome—rather amuses me." Then he drags me to the park. Which is where he always wants to go.

It may seem ridiculous for a grown man to be pulled around by a pug. But remember, Ollie weighs 25 pounds. And he's pretty muscle-bound for a little guy.

So I've returned to that alpha dog exercise which involves staring into his eyes and growling. Ollie seems mostly bored when I do this. No tangible signs of doggie submission yet.

Still, I am hopeful.

COVERT DOG SMUGGLING

One summer we smuggled Ollie the Pug (or as I now call him, Mr. X) into a beach-side cabin on one of the Gulf Islands.

It was a highly dangerous procedure, requiring tremendous tactical skills and nerves of tempered steel. You see, the proprietors of this cabin ordinarily do not allow dogs. They said Mr. X could come, but only if he slept outside.

"So … Ollie the Pug will be in a pup tent or something," I said to my wife.

"He might get eaten by raccoons," she said.

My wife then explained the necessity of embarking on a covert operation. She would bring the dog's crate and place it on the cabin's balcony, thus creating the impression Mr. X was bunking outside.

In reality, however, Mr. X would secretly be inside, engaging in his usual activities: breaking wind, snorting and shedding pounds of fur every time he shifted his sausage-like body.

The reality of smuggling in Mr. X was more difficult than one might imagine. For instance, when anyone knocked on the door, we embarked on a complicated procedure. My wife would grab Mr. X and dash into the bedroom. Then she'd put her hand over his mouth to keep him quiet.

One day, a locksmith came to the door. At least, he said he was a locksmith. He knocked. Mr. X barked loudly.

My wife seized Mr. X and sprinted to the bedroom. I opened the door slowly.

Locksmith: "Hi, I'm a locksmith. Just checking out the locks."

Me (suspiciously): "Oh … really?"

Locksmith, after a minute: "Well, the lock seems fine. Have a nice afternoon."

Me: "Oh, I will have a nice afternoon. Don't you worry about me."

My wife: "Why did you behave so strangely around the locksmith?"

Me: "Um … could have been a ruse."

My wife: "Because you know, if you act insanely every time someone comes to the door, they'll know something weird is going on."

Me: "I know. Let's have code names for each other. I will be the Wolf. You be the Penguin."

The Penguin: "No."

One day Ollie—I mean, Mr. X—made a bid for freedom. He started dashing about the area, dotted by other cabins. Then he did a pug run, sprinting about in a tight circle.

Other cabin folk reading trashy novels and sipping G&Ts regarded Mr. X curiously, no doubt thinking: "Hey … wait a minute. No dogs allowed. I must report this to the authorities."

I ran out and pretended Mr. X was a stray who'd wandered onto the dog-free holiday compound by mistake.

"Don't worry, I'll take care of this little guy," I said

loudly. "Wonder who he belongs to? Come here Ollie ... I mean, come here, you scamp, you."

It didn't help that Mr. X was wagging his tail madly and licking my face.

Mr. X loved the transition from urban dog to rural dog.

He cavorted leash-free on the beach. He saw another dog swimming and waddled in himself. He tried to bite a crab, which retaliated in a predictable manner.

On the day we left, my wife ordered a forensic cleanup of the cabin, to remove any trace of pug-dog-dom.

Thus I found myself on my knees with a Dustbuster in one hand and a lint-roller in the other, painstakingly removing hairs from the carpet.

It was a humbling experience. The fact that Mr. X kept leaping onto my head and biting my face only added to the excruciating pleasure.

Finally, we drove off. Mr. X, now secured safely in the back of the Volvo, whined and pawed at the window, as if to say, "Goodbye, goodbye! I must take my leave. Please remember me ... mostly by my trail of dog hairs."

All in all, it seemed Operation Ollie was a complete success.

"Good work, Penguin," I said to my wife. "Good work."

PET (AND HUMAN) FOIBLES

Dog owners love to discuss their pets' strange quirks. This is quite different from parents and their children.

Say you're the mother of two-year-old Rachel, who enjoys shoving beans up her nose at mealtimes. Well, you'd probably keep this idiosyncrasy under wraps.

That is, unless your kid is doing it right in front of everyone. Then you say, "Why little Rachel, stop that. You know, she's never done that before!" When in fact Rachel has inserted vegetable matter up her nasal cavities dozens of times.

But if your dog has foibles, why, they are happily discussed. Our pets' peccadilloes are probed, analyzed, celebrated. And if Fido is doing something peculiar at that very moment, most will interrupt important conversations to point it out.

Your best friend might be weepily revealing how his wife is contemplating leaving him, and you'll say: "How dire. Hey, check out my dog. He's trying to eat a spider!"

Here is one of Ollie the Pug's quirks. Scratch his hindquarters, he'll lick the pillows on the loveseats. There's no doubt bottom-scratching sends him into some rarefied state of ecstasy that can be increased only by simultaneous pillow-licking. Perhaps it's the pug-dog equivalent of the gentleman who enjoys a Cohiba cigar with his Talisker single malt.

Recently, a friend pointed me to an online forum called Pugslife ("a social network for pugs and their people") in which owners describe their pugs' unusual behaviours. Wrote one correspondent: "Daisy scares herself when she farts." Doesn't that paint a vivid picture in just a few words?

A fellow identifying himself as David Hall offered this one: "When I brought Zoe home she was eight weeks old and she slept in bed with me the first night so she would not be afraid and I awoke in the middle of the night to her suckling on my nipple!!"

Notice the use of double exclamation marks. Which, in this case, I believe are appropriate.

Another Pugslife contributor wrote about his pug, Otis. "He would sit down, put his front legs together and use his front legs as he might a female dog." It took me a minute to figure this one out. The description is as amusing as the quirk itself.

Other oddities are more familiar. One pug owner said her dog smelled "just like a sausage biscuit from McDonald's." This is like Ollie the Pug, who always smells like corn chips, even if he's just had a bath.

Pixie the Pug enjoys eating toilet paper, as does Ollie the Pug. And Gizmo likes sleeping on his owner's head, just like our dog. And if you scratch Ollie's hind-quarters while he's perched on top of your head, as an added bonus, he'll lick your ears.

More Ollie quirks:

He'll pummel the keys of the piano with his paws for treats.

He seems unable to recognize himself in a mirror.

He'll helpfully lick the water off your legs after you shower.

If you do sit-ups, he'll try to gnaw your face.

His tongue sticks out 90 per cent of the time.

Ollie the Pug is developing new idiosyncrasies. Yesterday morning, he was badly frightened upon noticing a black plastic bucket someone had discarded by our front gate. For about 30 seconds Ollie barked at it, while I tried to explain black plastic buckets constitute no real threat in the modern world.

We're happy to tell anyone about such foibles. But of course, if this were a child of ours, or some other relative, we'd keep it pretty quiet.

Imagine saying, "Uncle Fred licks the water off my legs after I shower." Or "Our daughter Julie, now a Harvard sophomore, scares herself each time she breaks wind."

You see what I mean? These are the sort of skeletons you'd want to keep in the closet.

PUG CARE PUNISHES
THE POCKETBOOK

Man, Ollie the Pug is costing me way too much dough. I mean, this is getting serious.

First off, he recently underwent dental surgery, which cost a bundle. Ollie needed a tooth pulled. No doubt it's a tricky operation requiring surgical tools fashioned from high-grade plutonium or something, as we ended up forking out $400.

And then Ollie went to the vet for a stomach ache. One morning, we found him lying forlornly on his bed, rather than scampering around as usual. He seemed all stiff. My wife even thought he felt cold.

Naturally we rushed him to the veterinarian. The vet confirmed the stomach-ache diagnosis. There was no blockage—an operation would not be necessary, she said. Hurray! Callooh, callay! Then she suggested taking X-rays. Sure, I said, take as many as you want. Fill your boots.

What I didn't realize is that each X-ray cost a sack o' cash. So at the end of that visit, we were out another $400. We've since bought pet medical insurance, needless to say. I didn't even know such a thing existed. And it's not cheap.

The latest Ollie expense is not as dire, but still cheeses me off. You see, I decided to buy Ollie a new doggie bed. He enjoys burrowing into the couches and the futon, which I'm not so crazy about because of the slobber factor. The cost of cleaning accumulated dog sputum from the couches and a futon came to a total of $300.

His old doggie bed was basically a mat, which is not so conducive to burrowing. I figured if I purchased a bed that was more burrow-worthy, it would save the couches and futon.

So I drove to this pet place and grabbed an olive-green doggie bed. The bed has really cushy-looking sides and a great big plumped-up pillow. It looked as if it would provide Mardis Gras-level opportunities for burrowing.

Alas, I did not examine the price tag. I mean, it was a dog bed, right? How expensive could it be?

The girl rang it up. And guess what? It was a hundred bucks. I mean, what is this, some kind of gold-plated doggie bed? But I was too embarrassed to say, "Hey, do you have any cheaper doggie beds that may not be as comfortable, but will sure help out with the old pocketbook?"

So I pulled out five twenties without comment.

Upon arriving home, my wife said, "Hey, nice doggie bed." And I said, "You're not kidding." But in a highly sarcastic tone, if you know what I mean. She said, "What's wrong?" and I said, "This doggie bed cost a hundred bucks. It must be gold-plated or something."

My wife grinned and examined the label. And get this— it is some kind of special Swedish doggie bed. You know, hand-crafted by the hard-working Swedes and all. Not only this, but it's advertised as "the best dog bed in the world." You can wash it repeatedly without fading. And it repels dog sputum, vomit and the like. It's made from a special fabric. Maybe space-age. Who knows.

This is all well and good. But I didn't really mean to buy Ollie the Pug the best dog bed known to man. We all love the little guy. But surely the second-best dog bed in the world would have sufficed. Jeez.

On the plus side, Ollie loves his Swedish space-age dog bed. Upon being presented with it, he immediately burrowed into the bed like an enthusiastic badger. No more couch-burrowing.

Well, at least not as much as before.

PUG DOG INTERPRETATION

The odd thing about dogs—and I imagine this extends to all pets—is how we assign human qualities to them.

This is technically known as anthropomorphism, although I prefer to call it "people being silly about their pets."

Last weekend, my wife took Ollie the Pug for a walk on Dallas Road. There she encountered another pug. A black one called Edward. Upon returning home, my wife told me Edward was so delighted to meet Ollie, he smiled.

"Dogs don't smile," I said. "Only people do that. And maybe orangutans. Like in that Clint Eastwood movie."

"Oh no," she said. "Edward did smile. And it was a nice, friendly pug smile."

Deep down, I knew that Edward did not smile. No doubt it was an involuntary grimace. Perhaps the dog was on the point of relieving itself. Our pug makes a peculiar, smile-like face when he does that.

But in marriage, one knows when to pursue a point, and when to back off. I backed off.

My wife also believes Ollie the Pug is a big-time smiler. "Look," she'll say. "Ollie's smiling. He's smiling because he's enjoying his TV show."

I'll look at Ollie. Not only will he be gazing away from

the television set, he will have exactly the same look on his face as always. This expression is one of perpetual worry, due to his furrowed brow and a downcast arrangement of the eyebrows. A habit of sticking out his tongue makes him look like a worried person who's rather dim. Sort of like that guy in Grade 9 math who'd constantly stick up his hand and say, "Um, sir … is this going to be on the test?"

Many of us believe our dogs understand us when we speak to them. They do, of course, to a certain extent. Words such as "sit," "come," "walkies" and "bad dog" can make sense to a pet. That is, after we repeat them two million times.

But what about those people who believe their dogs understand their elaborate, one-sided conversations? You know, the sort. "Hello, Fluffy, are you a good little dog? Did you have a nice day? And what's your opinion of the Helena Guergis scandal? What's that? Mr. Harper jumped the gun? Oh, you're so right."

This reminds me of an old *Far Side* cartoon. One panel shows a guy saying stuff to his dog. The other shows how the dog perceives his comments. "Blah blah blah, Fluffy. Blah, blah, blah."

Even worse are those who believe themselves in possession of a mysterious superpower: The ability to interpret their dog's innermost thoughts.

Let's take the scenario in which Buster the Bulldog stares uncomprehendingly at a spider.

"Buster says, 'Will I eat this spider? Or maybe I'll leave it alone,'" says his owner, pointing helpfully.

"Buster says, 'After all, the spider has a right to live.' He says, 'Mr. Spidee is one of God's creatures.' Isn't that right, Buster? Isn't that right?"

We've all overheard this kind of thing, right? I'm surprised there are not more dog-interpreter-related homicides.

This week we watched *The Wizard of Oz* at home. On my wife's lap sat Ollie the Pug.

"Ollie is watching," she said.

I looked over. His eyes were half closed.

"I don't think he's really watching."

"Yes, he is," said my wife. "See. Wow. He's so scared of those dancing midgets."

Ollie and I exchanged a look. And, do you know, I was suddenly blessed with that awesome ability to interpret his innermost thoughts.

"Hey, I'm a dog, not a human. I don't watch dancing midgets on TV," said Ollie the Pug telepathically. "I just want to sleep, eat and—just to make your life interesting—occasionally relieve myself on your new Turkish rug. Now go get me one of those fake bacon strips."

PUGS HAVE POWER
TO TEAR DOWN BARRIERS

The other day a tire on my daughter's car sprang a slow leak. Being an excellent father, I volunteered to get it repaired. Ollie the Pug came along, as any car trip fills him with delight.

I know zilch about fixing automobiles; to me, the internal combustion engine is a dark mystery. Upon entering any repair shop I am mystified and intimidated, in the manner of a Papua New Guinean tribesman touring an Apple computer factory. And of course repair guys—manly men by virtue of their trade—realize I know nothing. They can smell it on me: The foul pong of mechanical ignorance.

If I try to "talk the talk" they are not fooled for a second. I'll say something like, "Yeah, the car's been starting rough lately. I think it's the piston rod rubbing on the, um, lynch pin. Or perhaps a problem with 'the rad.'" There will be momentary silence, followed by gales of cruel laughter.

Anyway, I arrived at the tire place with Ollie in tow. Grease-stained men in overalls looked up at us. They regarded me as sommeliers might gaze upon someone toting a six-pack of malt liquor and a banjo.

Then one of them said, "Hey … is that Ollie?" It turned out this tire shop guy reads about Ollie in the newspaper.

Somehow, he recognized him—must have been his protruding tongue. The tire man became all friendly. He even gave Ollie several dog biscuits, much to the fat little pug's glee.

Bottom line: Having Ollie as my companion transformed what is normally a tiresome—and potentially unpleasant—task into a pretty fun event.

While the tire was being fixed, I took Ollie for a stroll down the street. It's an industrial-type area. On the corner sat a man, a woman and a dog. The woman was holding a enormous beer can. I prepared myself for mondo weirdness.

She looked at me, then said, "Hey, that's one f—ing cute dog!" And then she took a swig from her can. Which, upon closer inspection, turned out to be an energy drink, not beer.

How nice. Again, this was a small revelation. Thanks to Ollie, my preconceived ideas were proven wrong.

We made our way back to the tire shop. As we walked (with Ollie sniffing every tuft of grass) I noticed a guy in a used car lot wearing a white suit, a purple shirt and a white tie. He sidled between vehicles in our direction. Oh no, I thought to myself. God, please no.

The salesman, hair enthusiastically spiked like a pomaded porcupine, knelt down in front of Ollie. "Good boy, good boy. Oh, yes, you are a good boy," he said, patting the pug's head.

And then—get this—he allowed us to pass without trying to sell us a used Acura. This, to me, was almost unbelievable.

When we re-entered the tire shop, Ollie's admirer explained to everyone that this was Ollie the Pug from the newspaper. True, the other tire guys did not seem particularly impressed. Still, I left the shop with a spring in my step.

Driving home (with Ollie trying to bite my face instead of sitting in his seat) I pondered the tire man, the beer-can lady and the spikey-haired car salesman. Each time, my preconceptions were proven wrong. Could it be that most people are actually, well … nice? My lifelong philosophy of mild misanthropism was shaken somewhat.

Not to sound too New Age-y or anything, but walking around with Ollie often seems like wearing a magical cloak that attracts friendly vibes. And that, as convicted criminal Martha Stewart used to say, is a good thing.

PUG LOVERS AND
NON-PUG LOVERS

Be nice to my super friendly dog or I won't like you.

Of late, I've noticed that some people react poorly when Ollie the Pug dashes up to them and licks their faces—or whatever other body part is reachable with his extraordinarily long tongue.

Such folk are aghast at the sight of a pug dog waddling toward them. They gasp in horror. They cling their children tightly to their breasts. Their whole aspect says, "Oh, for the love of God, save me from that beast!"

Such a reaction would be super appropriate if a Bengal tiger was on the loose. Boy, if I saw a Bengal tiger, I'd make a run for it, believe me. Indeed, in my vigorous effort to flee, I'd shove you into some prickly bushes.

But pug dogs are not tigers. They (the pug dogs, that is) are affectionate and mostly harmless creatures. They have wrinkly, pushed-in muzzles. They are roly-poly. Who flees at the sight of anything roly-poly?

My motto, to restate, is this: Be nice to my super-friendly dog or I won't like you.

I divide human race into two categories. Firstly, there are the pug lovers.

Such folk are tolerant and kind. They are invariably far

more attractive, physically speaking, than the average person. They wear colour co-ordinated linen outfits in exquisite earth tones. If you spill boiling hot coffee on your lap in a public place, the pug lover will immediately spill his or her boiling hot coffee on his or her lap. Just to keep you company and all. In fact, we have protective aprons sewn into our clothing for just such an eventuality.

Then there are those who dislike pugs. The non-pug-lovers. Such folk—while not wholly evil—inhabit a world closer to the dark side. They tend to be crafty, with a penchant for lurking in doorways at night. If you're in line at Starbucks, it is the non-pug-lover who surreptitiously slips ahead of you using moves gleaned from hot-yoga classes. Their CD collection is weighted heavily in favour of *American Idol* winners and Enya. They laugh loudly at their own taste-less jokes and mispronounce the word "nuclear."

Barack Obama is a dyed-in-the-wool pug lover. Whereas Sarah Palin detests pugs. In fact, if she sees one, her reaction is akin to someone encountering a Bengal tiger.

At the risk of becoming tiresome, let me say once again: Be nice to my super-friendly dog. Or I won't like you.

Once, on a walk, I encountered a non-pug-lover (or NPL) who had the frightened Bengal tiger reaction upon seeing Ollie the Pug. Recovering, she then pretended to be a pug-lover (or PL), kneeling down to examine him.

"What a fat little dog! Oh, you're a little fattie! And why is your tongue sticking out in that silly way!" she exclaimed, tapping Ollie the Pug's head as though testing a melon for ripeness.

What cheek. Thank heavens Ollie has no understanding

of the English language, other than "supper," "walkies" and "who's that?" How would this NPL have liked it had I said to her, "What extraordinarily unflattering sweat-pants you are wearing. Were you by any chance waylaid on the way to a fire sale at a discount department store?"

Or "Your exuberant use of makeup, combined with that ghastly bottle-blond hairdo, gives you the hard, artificial look of an aging hostess at a gentleman's club that, while reasonably popular in the late 1970s, has now fallen on desperately hard times."

So be nice to my super-friendly dog, or … well, you know.

PUG MIRACLES

During these dark days—what with dire predictions of global warming and American politics getting nuttier by the minute—we need all the feel-good stories we can get.

Therefore, I present ... the uplifting tale of Penny the Miracle Pug.

Val Crossley of Brentwood Bay tipped me to the story. Her relatives, who live in the Yukon, recently acquired a pug puppy. Such a choice was a surprise, as these folk ordinarily select breeds more suitable to Canada's northern climate. As Val puts it: "Prior dogs in the family were appropriately Yukon-esque breeds with wolf-like physical characteristics and disposition, and probably a goodly mix of feral canine genes." Tellingly, their other animal is named Jack the Eskimo Dog.

Her relatives chose a pug because the breed is supposedly good with children. Sadly, this backfired when the family's granddaughter refused to play with the pug (which they named Penny) because the child found it too ugly.

One day, Penny the Homely Pug and Jack the Eskimo Dog accompanied the family to Tagish Lake, outside of Whitehorse. Suddenly, when everyone's back was turned, Penny mysteriously disappeared into the wilds. The family searched for hours, even days, but could not find the pup.

They decided Penny was lost for good, as eight-month-old pugs don't usually do well in the Yukon wilderness. There are grizzlies, coyotes, wolves, birds of prey … not to mention the cold.

Nine days later, guess who turns up? Yes. Penny the Pug. Someone found her walking through a graveyard a few kilometres from where she got lost. Penny was wearing her little grey plaid coat, which might have kept her alive.

"Penny is now home, safe and sound, a little skinnier (apparently her wrinkles have disappeared but no ribs showing—bless that puggish predisposition to an extra layer of subcutaneous fat) perpetually hungry and presumably less inclined to wander," wrote Val.

Wow.

This brought to mind my own special encounter with a dog hero.

The other weekend, Ollie the Pug and I went to a pet fair in Saanich. The event was specifically for rescue-dog societies.

One rescue dog in attendance was Super Chick the Wonder Dog. Super Chick was rescued from the mean streets of Tai Cjung. When found, her back legs were so badly damaged, veterinarians were forced to amputate. Then, for some reason, she was shipped off to Canada for adoption.

Here's the amazing thing about Super Chick. She's somehow able to walk around on her two front legs. She suspends the back half of her body in the air. It's a bit like those gymnasts who walk on their hands.

You'd think Super Chick would be depressed, lacking

her back legs and all. Not at all. She is a very happy dog, according to the information posted at the fair. Indeed, the write-up said Super Chick is so persistently cheerful, she was even happy during her leg removal process.

Imagine that. Certainly the trials and tribulations of Super Chick put us all to shame. Let's say, for example, you get annoyed upon getting cut off in traffic by rude drivers. But imagine if you had no legs! Perhaps you are vexed by long movie lineups. But imagine if you had no legs! It puts everything in perspective, you see.

Ollie did not seem particularly interested in Super Chick, despite her irrepressible cheeriness. But he did enjoy playing with another rescue dog with three legs. His name is Tripod.

Driving home with Ollie the Pug and my wife, I wondered aloud why Super Chick was named Super Chick.

"I guess it's because he looks like a chicken," I said. "Because he walks on two legs, in the manner of a chicken."

"Don't be silly," said my wife. "It's a girl dog. That's where the 'chick' part comes in. It's nothing to do with chickens."

To amuse myself, I paid homage to Super Chick the Wonder Dog by singing a song about her. It was really the Rudolph the Red-Nosed Reindeer song. But instead of being about Rudolph, my version was about Super Chick, her happy nature and her ability to walk on two legs.

After a minute or two, my wife made me stop singing the Super Chick song, though.

PUGS AND MENTAL HEALTH

I've often wondered whether dogs suffer from a rich cornucopia of mental ailments, just as we humans do.

Our family sometimes takes Ollie the Pug to a grassy field near our home. Owners regularly bring their dogs to this park for the purpose of cavorting.

There is, however, one dog of indeterminate breed who never plays with the others. I believe his name is Lucky. The unfortunate Lucky will do only one thing—chase a soccer ball around the field, nosing it around with his snout. It is far removed from the bottom-sniffing-centred hijinx enjoyed by the others. Dogs, I mean.

If a human spent hours chasing a soccer ball, he would be classed as obsessive compulsive. Unless he was a soccer player or something. So if Lucky is indeed obsessive compulsive, what else lies out there in dog-land? Self-loathing dogs? Pyromaniacal dogs? Dogs plagued by imaginary voices saying "Walkies!" or "Bath time!"?

I just read an article that says dogs—especially Dobermans—can indeed suffer from obsessive compulsive disorders just as humans do. In the case of Dobermans, this typically manifests itself in sucking their flanks and/or blankets.

So how does Ollie the Pug fit into the flank-sucking picture? Well, if our family goes for a car ride and one of us exits the vehicle—say to get something from the drugstore—Ollie goes completely bonkers. He howls, whines and presses his face against the window until the missing party returns.

In fact, Ollie goes so berserk, I suggested to my wife we follow the example of Temple Grandin. Temple is the celebrated autistic writer who, as a teenager, would squeeze herself in a cattle press in order to quell her anxiety. And it worked like a charm. So why not construct a pug-sized version of the Temple Grandin press in my workshop?

However, my wife deemed this idea as (1) unworkable and (2) completely insane.

I've also noticed Ollie the Pug has a terribly poor memory. For example, he has been told about 1,000 times not to chew his smelly bones on the couches. However, almost every day he'll leap up on the couch for a good chew. If you tell him to get down, he seems surprised and hurt. I wonder if this is symptomatic of some profound mental impairment, such as early dog dementia.

Then again, the same might be said for myself. For instance, I often brush my teeth in the morning, then forget whether I've brushed my teeth. I have to feel my toothbrush to see if it's wet.

I asked my wife whether this was a harbinger of Alzheimer's disease. She assured me it's just absent-mindedness. But I'm not so sure.

Similarly, I often fail to remember people I've previously met. Sometimes such folk want to chat. I can tell from the tenor of the conversation that we are acquaintances of some sort. The problem is, I cannot remember anything, including their names.

So what I do is pretend to know what's going on. This "go with the flow" approach is pretty successful in masking mental lapses.

Of course, if people say, "Hey, do you remember the time we did such and such?" then it doesn't work so well. And if they say, "Hey, do you even know what my name is?" the whole house of cards collapses.

Still, everyone's got a few quirks. We're learning to accept Ollie's foibles. Although I still think the Temple Grandin press for pug dogs might be worth trying.

PUGS IN THE
GREAT OUTDOORS

By now, most of us have heard about Bob the Wonder Pug and the wolf.

For those who haven't—possibly distracted by lesser news such as the Afghanistan election fraud and the Vatican scandal—here is the lowdown. Bob is a pug dog abducted from his backyard in Prince Rupert by a wolf. His heroic owners, one wielding a hockey stick, chased the wolf and saved Bob.

Rescuer Courtney Scott bravely leapt over an embankment and fell down front first. She offered a *Vancouver Sun* reporter this magnificent quote:

"I landed on my poor boobs and I just had a baby." (I had to read this twice before I understood what she meant.)

What interested me most, though, were a couple of lines at the end of a story. It suggested Bob the Wonder Pug survived the wolf attack only because he has "tons of skin." In other words, it was difficult for the wolf to get sufficient purchase on Bob's neck, because it's so fat.

For me, this was terrific news. You see, Ollie the Pug is also blessed with a copious amount of neck skin. His neck is so voluminous, my daughter's friend says it makes his face resemble a bowl of stirred batter.

To my mind, Ollie's flesh curtain resembles an Elizabethan ruff, the sort Shakespeare wore to opening nights. So if a wolf runs out to grab him, he'll spend so much time trying to find dog under the ruff, it'll give my wife sufficient time to rescue him (and provide me the opportunity to make my escape, shrieking like a prepubescent girl).

Of course, in the Chamberlain household, the main wildlife fear isn't wolves. It's eagles and hawks. We often take Ollie for a walk in a nearby field. I figure, to birds of prey hovering above, he resembles a furry kielbasa or a hirsute bratwurst.

Could Ollie be swooped away? In 2002, CNN reported Ava the dachshund was seized by a bald eagle in Maine. The bird carried the six-kilogram dog 90 metres in the air before dropping it. Amazingly, the pet survived.

Other predator versus dog attacks:

- In Lake Mary, Fla., Gator the lab was killed by a bear.
- In northern Australia, Bindi the terrier was gobbled up by a python.
- In Fairfield, Calif., a teenager said a mountain lion attacked his dog. Upon inspecting the animal's tracks, it was determined the mountain lion was in fact an enormous raccoon.

Sometimes the tables are turned. Remember the uplifting story from early this year, in which Angel the golden retriever saved an 11-year-old boy from being devoured by a cougar near Boston Bar?

In truth, I cannot imagine Ollie the Pug saving me in this manner. Ollie would presume the cougar was just a big dog. And he'd no doubt try to make friends with it. At which point the cougar would swallow the furry kielbasa in one or two gulps. And then he'd turn his attention to yours truly, the main course (unless, of course, the process of devouring Ollie affords me the opportunity to make my escape, shrieking like a prepubescent girl).

A GAY OLD TIME

Last Sunday, my wife told me she had an irresistible desire to attend the Big Gay Dog Walk.

I didn't know what this was. She said it is a annual dog walk sponsored by the Victoria Pride Society.

It sounded, well … very good. Very good indeed.

There was just one problem.

"I don't think Ollie is gay," I said. "And he's pretty small."

To be honest, I was not 100 per cent sure of the veracity of either statement. Ollie now weighs 25 pounds, which makes him heavier than most pug dogs. So while he isn't "big"—as in German Shepherd or Labrador Retriever big—he's certainly on the chubby side.

In addition, during several pug meet-ups, I've noticed that one dog, Winston, makes a habit of mounting Ollie. So does his pal Elvis (the pug dog, not the late entertainer).

Certainly, our dog seemed more or less oblivious to these overtures. But then again, he didn't reject them, either. So does such activity make our dog, well … gay?

Happily, it turned out my fretting was for naught. My wife explained the Big Gay Dog Walk isn't for gay dogs. Rather, it's a gay-friendly event in which Victoria citizens of all sexual preferences walk their pets.

Participants are encouraged to dress up their dogs. And

for my wife, this was the main appeal. She loves dog costumes fiercely. How much? Let's just say she once purchased a toddler's bumble-bee outfit from London Drugs—complete with antennae—and squeezed Ollie into it for Halloween.

So my daughter, my wife and I set out Sunday afternoon with Ollie to participate in the Big Gay Dog Walk, which happened on Dallas Road. For the occasion, our dog wore a red and white ruffle around his neck, which made him look like a furry harlequin.

The Big Gay Dog Walk turned out to be jolly as all get-out. The sun shone; Abba blasted on a stereo system. A wiener dog pranced about in rainbow-coloured Hawaiian leis.

Another pet was costumed as a pink fairy. Also seen in passing: a pug in a black motorcycle jacket, a dog wearing an enormous multicoloured bow tie, a man sporting angel wings, a woman in a green corset and ripped fishnets, and a woman in a red corset leading another by a silver chain.

Oh, and get this. There was some guy walking around with a ferret! The things some people do in public.

Because the event's focus was mostly on dogs wearing funny costumes, it gave folk—friends and strangers alike—something in common to talk about.

There was an all-round atmosphere of tolerance and acceptance—everyone seemed to be having tremendous fun.

"What a marvellous thing this Big Gay Dog Walk is," I thought to myself. "There's something irresistibly playful about its name, which somehow acts as a soothing societal balm."

After we returned from the BGDW, my thoughts returned to Ollie, Winston, Elvis and those hedonistic pug meet-ups.

Digging around, I found a recent *New York Times* article, "Can Animals Be Gay?" It said scientists have recorded same-sex activity in about 450 species to date. For instance, they once observed a female koala mounting another female and emitting "exalted, belchlike sounds."

Can it be being gay is just a natural thing, enjoyed by koalas, pug dogs and 448 other species?

Ollie, exhausted after his Big Gay Dog Walk, was sound asleep on his mat. I found his colourful harlequin ruffle and gently placed it back around his neck.

"Ollie," I said softly, "your doggie lifestyle choices are your own. Which ever way you roll, the Chamberlain family supports you, 100 per cent."

SUSPICIOUS WET SPOTS

At first, I thought Ollie the Pug was drinking too much.

It seemed every time you looked, fluid dribbled from his jaw. I figured Ollie was hitting the ol' water dish. Often. And hard.

Our pug dog has gone on the occasional bender in the past, gulping like a man who's crossed the Kalahari in mid-summer. And, like most of us, he spews if he overindulges.

So what was at the root of Ollie's out-of-control drinking? Women problems? Trouble at work? Anger over his supply of chicken-broth-dipped rawhide sticks running out?

"Go easy there, little guy," I advised. "She ain't worth it. No dame is. Ditto for the rawhide sticks."

Ollie the Pug gazed at me blankly. His tongue was hanging out. Water dribbled down.

One morning, my wife found Ollie snoring on the couch. There was a large round patch of fluid on the fabric. At first, she thought he had relieved himself. Upon closer inspection, it was evident that was not the case.

Ollie arose, shook himself, ran into the bedroom and leapt onto the bed. Which contained yours truly. It wasn't a particularly welcome wake-up call. Once again, water cascaded from his mouth a veritable Niagara Falls.

Like a very-slow-on-the-uptake Sherlock Holmes, I

finally clued in. This wasn't excess water-drinking. It was pug drool.

Like any right-minded citizen fortunate enough to live in this electronic age, I turned to the Internet for wisdom and advice. Excessive dog drool, I learned, can be a symptom of dental problems. Or something stuck in the dog's mouth. Or even poisoning.

Worried, we took him to the vet. Naturally, by the time Ollie got there, there was no drooling. Absolutely zilch. He seemed just fine. Entering the lobby, Ollie strained madly on his leash, desperate to play with all the sick animals. Cats, dogs, parakeets. All creatures great and small, this pug dog loves them all.

The vet hoisted Ollie on the table and gave him a thorough prodding. He passed. She peered into his mouth. That was OK, too.

Then she attempted to insert a thermometer.

Apparently, if you're a dog, this is not an oral procedure. "He's puckering," she noted.

Hey, if I were Ollie, I'd be puckering, too.

Finally, the vet said Ollie seemed healthy. Probably no need for a blood test. She suggested, if the drooling resumed, that we could take a sample of his "morning urine."

How exactly would that work, I wondered? Well, just like this. You take your dog out first thing in the morning. Then, with vial in hand, you swoop in to catch the first offering of the day.

Not a big deal, really. After all, I was already swooping in with little biodegradable plastic bags to retrieve other offerings. Still, this new development took me aback.

Would plastic gloves be involved? Would I look insane to passersby? Where would it all end?

Little did I know, upon adopting Ollie the Pug two years ago, that my manservant duties would extend so very, very far.

"Well," I said, after a second's reflection. "I'm sure Ollie is A-OK. Look. His excessive drooling seems to have completely stopped. No need for the urine sampling. Hooray!"

Ollie does seem back to his old self. Last Sunday, terribly excited after his weekly bath, he undertook a crazed pug run around the house. Ollie leapt onto the couch and knocked the martini right out of my hand.

Two jalapeno-stuffed olives rolled across the floor. Hardly missing a step, he devoured both—skilfully puck-handling them with his tongue. I did not mind at all. For surely, this is mark of a healthy and happy dog.

THE MERITS OF PUGS, AS OPPOSED TO "REAL MEN'S" DOGS

My old college friend Darryl dropped by on the weekend. And, as is so often the case, he gave me a hard time.

Darryl takes great pleasure in dispensing unsolicited advice on all subjects. These observations are presented as cold, hard truths. He is happiest when pointing out things (usually character faults or minor physical defects) that others are too dull-witted to notice without his help.

On this particular day, Darryl lectured me on my choice of dog.

"Why did you buy that stupid pug?" is what he said.

Ollie the Pug gazed at him uncomprehendingly, wagging his tail so hard his bottom wiggled. Ollie's I mean, not Darryl's.

"Because I happen to like pug dogs," I said.

"Like? What do you mean, like? Pug dogs are lap dogs. Why didn't you get a proper man's dog, like a German shepherd, a husky or possibly an English mastiff?"

"Because I don't want some enormous dog jumping up and down and knocking over all my furniture," I said. "Besides, pugs are fine, sociable creatures."

Darryl had finished eating the ham sandwich my wife made him for lunch. So he took half of mine and bit into it with relish.

"There's plenty of reasons not to buy a pug," he said, moving his jaws vigorously.

"Name three."

"Well, inbreeding for starters. That's why your dog's snout is all smashed-in looking. Like he ran into a wall."

Ollie walked slowly underneath Darryl's chair. He snorted noisily—in that laboured, I'm-on-my-last-breath way pugs have—sniffing for crumbs.

"As well, his legs are all stunted," Darryl said. "You can't go for a proper run with a pug."

"You can," I said. "But it has be a short one. Like for half a block or something."

"Precisely my point," he said. "Not a proper run. Whereas with an English mastiff—oh noble creature—you can jog for hours. You could run through farmers' fields— the sort that are replete with golden wheat, rippled by gentle summer breezes. You could even run a marathon."

"When's the last time you ran a marathon?" I asked.

My friend shoved a square of fudge cake into his mouth. Ollie, noticing a new rain of crumbs, snorted harder. He commenced bobbing and weaving around crazily, like Jake Lamotta, licking the floor.

Darryl responded, but due to a debilitating cake blockage, it just sounded like "Nom, nom, nom." After a moment or two, he spoke again.

"And what about protection? You know, household protection."

"What about it? If a stranger walks up the garden path, Ollie barks like a nutter."

"But when I came in the door, he just wagged his tail

and licked my hands," said Darryl.

"Yeah. But he knows you."

Ollie, having hoovered the last particles of fudge cake, was now asleep and snoring noisily. He had placed his chin on my foot, to use as a pillow.

"That's why you want a big dog. Like a German shepherd. If a burglar comes in, those dogs go for the throat, like for the carotid artery. With the German shepherd, it's always a fight to the death."

To emphasize the words "fight to the death," Darryl waved a piece of cake with theatrical vigour, in the manner of Toscanini conducting *La bohème* at La Scala. A piece fell off. Ollie opened an eye, spied the fallen cake and wolfed it down.

I moved the cake dish away from Darryl. "But I'm not that crazy about hosting fights to the death in my house."

"That doesn't surprise me at all," he said. "When it comes to the crunch, guys who buy pug dogs cannot withstand acts of physical violence. You'd make an awful cowboy or hip-hop gangsta."

My wife entered the room.

"By the way, Darryl, do you still have that cute little cat?"

"Yes," he said after a moment.

"What's his name again?"

"Um, Mr. Puffy," said Darryl, standing up. "I'd better be going."

I walked my old college friend to the door, then bid him adieu.

"Thanks for dropping by," I said, waving. "Say hi to Mr. Puffy for me."

Darryl didn't hear me, I guess. At least, he didn't turn around.

THE PIED PIPER OF
PANAMA FLATS

The other day I took Ollie the Pug for a walk on Panama Flats. The flats are a large, pretty field, providing a habitat for herons, ducks, swans and the like.

Ollie trotted along off-leash several metres in front of me, his bottom wiggling merrily. Suddenly, he dashed back in my direction. He was being chased by a furry, greyish beast.

The poor pug was so frightened he leapt into my arms, whimpering. His pursuer stopped in its tracks and glared.

It was an enormous rat.

Startled, I waved my walking stick. The rat scowled for a moment. I tossed the stick in its direction. It nipped into a dense thicket of blackberry bushes and disappeared.

"What do you think you're doing?" someone yelled.

I turned to meet the gaze of tall man in his mid-20s. He wore rubber boots (patterned in an unusual manner) and a Tilley hat and sported a pony-tail.

"Oh, don't worry. I think it scared my dog a little. But it's gone now," I said.

"You are brutalizing a defenceless animal. I ought to report you. How'd you like it if I threw a stick at you?"

I studied the man's face for signs of derangement. But

he looked normal enough. Although he did have a funny little squib of facial hair under his lower lip.

"It's just a rat," I said. "It was after my dog."

"Just a rat? Rats are one of God's creatures, my friend. They have rights, just as you and I do. They have dreams and ambitions. They have families. They fall in love."

Almost without thinking, I said, "There are too many rats in this field. They do a lot of damage. There should be a … you know. A rat cull or something."

"A rat cull? What—kind—of—a—human—being—are—you?" said the man. He pulled his flannel shirt open, revealing a T-shirt that read: "Rat Defenders of Vancouver Island." At this point, I made out the pattern on his rubber boots. Little cartoon rats engaged in various pursuits. One was riding a unicycle.

Now fully realizing my predicament, I called to Ollie and prepared to make a hasty exit. But the Tilley-hatted rat defender wouldn't let me leave.

"Rats get a bum rap from people like you," he said. "They are a much misunderstood species. In fact, rats are friendly, curious and make wonderful pets."

"Oh, really?" I said.

"Rats have metacognition abilities, just like humans," the man continued.

"And there are many positive examples of rats in popular culture. Take, for example, Ratty in *Wind in the Willows*. Ratty was a tremendous help to Mole and displayed a deep and abiding love of the river and surrounding habitat."

Ollie growled softly at the man. And I confess, he was making me nervous.

"Wasn't Ratty a vole?" I said.

The man frowned.

"Look bud," said the Tilley-hatted man. "I shouldn't really tell you this, but the Rat Defenders of Vancouver Island are spearheading an effort to save the rats of Panama Flats. I know they're under attack by heartless dog owners such as you. Next week we're sending 500 rats to a rescue sanctuary. In Hickory Ridge, Arkansas. They will be transported in air-conditioned trucks. Equipped with hamster exercise wheels. And plenty of cheeses, including some choice asiago mezzanno and gorgonzola. It's going to cost $50,000."

And then the rat man, holding out his palm, asked, "Will you contribute?"

The only bill in my wallet was a twenty. I handed it over. After all, this fellow was getting rid of rats. Last winter, one infiltrated our house and then died. I found its dried corpse in our basement, tucked in our artificial Christmas tree. A macabre Yuletide ornament.

As the man pocketed my bill, Ollie and I made a bolt for it.

We ran so quickly, we almost bumped into a stooped, mud-caked man pushing a shopping cart containing his meagre belongings.

He asked if I could spare any change.

"I'm sorry, I cannot," I said, "having spent my last bit of cash to send 500 rats on permanent vacation to Arkansas in an air-conditioned truck."

"Makes sense," said the homeless man.

"Arf," said Ollie the Pug.

THE THERAPEUTIC EFFECT
OF A RUN WELL DONE

My wife wanted to take Ollie the Pug to the GoodLife Fitness Victoria Marathon. And what's worse, she wanted him to wear his new costume.

She has a thing about stuffing Ollie into dumb outfits. Last Halloween she dressed him as a bee.

This time she bought him a pig costume. It's a knitted, handmade thing. On the back is a great big pig's face. It looks absolutely insane.

"No," I said. "You can't bring him. He'll get trampled. Plus he looks like a nut in that pig getup."

She was insistent. So we compromised. Ollie could come, but no pig costume.

My daughter and I had enrolled for the half-marathon part of the event. She's a keen runner. She trained and everything. I didn't train so much, wanting to conserve my energy for the big day.

We drove downtown and parked. Ollie strained excitedly on his leash, yanking us along as though we were his pets. As we passed the Fairmont Empress hotel, an old man pointed at our dog and smiled delightedly.

"Vat is his name?" said the man, who sounded German.

"Ollie," said my wife.

"Ali Baba!" he exclaimed. And then he pointed to Ollie's pig-like tail and made a mysterious swirling motion with his finger.

Unsettling, somehow. Of course, I was in a terrible mood. We had arisen at an ungodly hour to make the 7:30 a.m. start time. Plus, to be honest, I'm always in a mildly bad mood.

That morning everything bugged me. At the start line, for instance, there were runners wearing garbage bags. I guess they were just trying to keep warm, but they looked like numbskulls. All the half-marathoners were in tremendously good spirits, back-slapping and bobbing up and down. It was like an Up With People convention for people wearing tight shorts.

The start signal sounded. Sort of a let down. We were in the middle of the pack, and so had to wait several minutes to even start running.

As the race progressed, the throng thinned out. My daughter zoomed ahead of me. I found myself loping along with joggers of all shapes, sizes and ages. The mediocre runners. I relaxed, for these are my people.

A fellow runner, an office-mate, noticed I had an iPod. She asked what I was listening to. In fact, it was 'I Want You Back' by the Jackson Five. But revealing this seemed uncool. I considered shouting, "It's 'I'm Waiting for the Man' by the Velvet Underground!" but instead just said, "Um, you know. A variety of stuff."

Part of the half-marathon route was hairpin loop. So, after a time, we encountered elite half-marathoners sprinting down the other side of the road. Seeing them lapping us like this was humiliating.

What's worse, instead of making rude gestures at the pack leaders, the runners around me starting cheering and clapping.

I don't want to come off as the Half-Marathon Grinch, but even the spectators cheering us on got on my nerves. Some rang giant cow bells. One guy blew a conch. They sat in lawn chairs, snuggled underneath cosy blankets. Where was my cosy blanket? Why wasn't I sitting and watching, cradling a Starbucks latté, instead of running around like a knob?

At about 15 kilometres my thighs started to chafe badly. My irritation grew. At 18 kilometres, we passed more well-wishers. It was a gaggle of elderly ladies dressed as cheerleaders, dancing to hits from the 1960s. God. Seeing these seniors kick out the jams to "Woolly Bully" wasn't helping my thighs any.

Finally, the half-marathon was over. It was the farthest I'd ever run. But my pride soon gave way to annoyance once again. We runners were gated in what appeared to be a jumbo cattle pen. As more half-marathoners finished, the crush grew intense. The situation was worsened by the fact many runners were enthusiastically chowing down at a pastry tent, thus blocking my exit. Typical, I thought. Do something healthy, then ruin it all by gobbling down deep-fried crullers.

My daughter, who had finished a full 10 minutes before me, was elated by the experience. Her enthusiasm rubbed off on me. Hey, at least I'd finished without having a heart attack. As we drove home, my wife began planning that evening's Thanksgiving dinner.

"And tonight, Ollie can wear his pig costume," she declared happily.

"Great," I said.

"Dad," warned my daughter.

"No, that's great. Seriously."

A new, weird feeling had come over me. I hate to admit it, but the Half-Marathon Grinch was feeling, well … rather good.

WADDLE SOFTLY AND
CARRY A SMALL STICK

One Sunday afternoon, we took Ollie the Pug to the beach. To say he was outclassed by the bigger dogs is an understatement.

I'd spent that morning gardening. At our house, "gardening" is a euphemism for pulling moss out of the lawn. Ollie is not allowed to join me in the yard, as he might make a dash for freedom. So, as I yanked moss, Ollie regarded me from the front window, his face forlorn in typical pug fashion.

I felt sorry for the little tyke.

"Let's take Ollie to the beach," I said to my wife.

There's a beach at Saxe Point favoured by dog owners. Dogs romp off-leash, sniffing the balmy sea breeze and savagely biting kelp bulbs. When we arrived, a plaid-jacketed fellow was cavorting in a manly fashion with his German shepherd.

Ollie immediately dashed over. He likes all big dogs. Perhaps he imagines that he, too, is a big dog.

The German shepherd ignored Ollie. That's because his owner was flinging a stick in the sea for him to fetch. The German shepherd would swim out, no matter how far the stick was thrown.

Impressive? Oh, yes. For to call this stick a "stick" is the understatement of the decade, akin to describing Nancy Grace as "somewhat annoying" or Charlie Sheen as "not really the greatest husband." In fact, the stick was a small log. It must have weighed 30 pounds.

The bearded dog-owner would heave his mighty pole into the sea with a testosterone-fuelled grunt, in the manner of those kilt-wearing Scottish fellows who enjoy hurling small trees for sport.

The German shepherd would then fling itself into the churning surf, dog-handle the log back to shore, then shake itself vigorously, flinging plumes of spray in every direction.

Ollie watched with great interest. Once—but only once—he tried to bite the other dog's log. The German shepherd lunged forward with great ferocity, barking savagely at his approach. Ollie scurried back to me with a worried look on his face, no doubt fearing for his very life.

I tossed a twig—about the size of a chopstick—for Ollie to play with. He chased it a little, but alas, his heart wasn't in it. He gazed yearningly at the German shepherd, as if to say: "Oh, to be able to chomp on a log like that giant dog! To be able to swim the foamy waters of the great Pacific Ocean! Alas, I am just a chubby pug, the same general shape as a wienerwurst, only a good deal rounder."

A woman with a large boxer (I mean a dog, not a pugilist) arrived. She, too, began to fling logs into the sea. Perhaps this is a time-honoured Saxe Point tradition.

Then the woman started yelling at the boxer. I guess the dog wasn't retrieving his log correctly or something. It was sort of awful, like being in the middle of a domestic dispute in which people express anger by throwing lumber.

"Come on, Ollie," I said. "This is no place for the likes of us."

Ollie wagged his curled tail and bit a kelp bulb. And then he followed me, quite happily, up the path back to the car.

WEIRD DOG BEHAVIOUR
SUDDENLY MAKES SENSE

The whole idea of teaching dogs tricks seems odd to me.

Sure, instruct your dog to pee outdoors and stay off your bed. But these aren't tricks, are they? They're useful learned behaviours. Whereas teaching Fido to fall to the floor after you pretend your hand is a handgun is merely a silly gag designed to follow the phrase: "Hey guys, get a load of this."

Enter my wife who, every day, patiently coaches Ollie the Pug to do various tricks. Yes, he has learned some, including rolling over and playing the piano. The latter is Ollie bounding up to our upright and boxing the keys tunelessly with this paws, desperate for a Nutty Nanner treat.

I was reminded of the dog-trick issue upon reading *Inside of a Dog*, an excellent book by Alexandra Horowitz.

If you're interested in dogs I recommend this *New York Times* best-seller, as Horowitz possesses both keening smarts (a PhD in cognitive science) and writing ability (she was a staffer on the *New Yorker*).

She tells the story of Rico, who's some sort of genius border collie. If asked, he can select any one of more than 200 toys by name.

Aside from the rather disturbing fact that Rico's owners

purchased him 200-plus toys, this über-feat puts my wife's dog trickery to shame.

You see, she's been trying to teach Ollie to select either his pig toy or his squirrel toy on command. Despite dozens of attempts, our dog just seizes his pig or his squirrel randomly, then gazes around with goggle-eyed mania, desperate for a Nutty Nanner. Rico's record is obviously in no danger from Ollie, who (in my more uncharitable moments) reminds me one of those affable but very dim friends with whom you cut class in high school.

I know the problem, of course. For Ollie the Pug, "Get your pig!" or "Get your squirrel!" sounds like "blah de blah" and "blah de blah-blah." Despite our romantic anthropomorphic notions, dogs don't truly comprehend language or mathematics as humans do. This is backed up by Horowitz, who suggests the following experiment. Instead of saying "Go for a walk" to your dog in the morning, say "snow 40 locks." If you use the same tone of voice, the dog will bound up, ready for his leash.

Now, when my wife attempts the pig/squirrel toy trick, I chime in helpfully with "Get your wig!" and "Spot the plural!" Not to mention "Snap the twig!" and "Gott im Himmel!"

Alas, she is oddly unappreciative of my efforts, even when I patiently explain they are inspired by a best-selling cognitive scientist with a superior writing style.

Indeed, Horowitz's keen scientific mind has sliced through Chamberlain doggie-dom like a straight-razor.

For instance, we had believed Ollie was "kissing" us when, upon our return home, he licks our faces. In fact, according to Horowitz, he's doing what wolf puppies do with their mothers. She writes: "Licking around the mouth seems to be the cue that stimulates her [the wolf mother] to vomit up nicely partially digested meat."

So far, Ollie has been disappointed in his quest. But at least we know what he's really after.

Horowitz has also cleared up other doggie mysteries. For instance, open hearing a car door slam in our driveway, Ollie will leap up to the front window.

Yet as we walk up the front path, yelling "Hi Ollie!" and waving, he stares at us blankly, seeming not to "see" us even though we're just five metres away.

In fact, he may not. Horowitz says short-nosed dogs like pugs lack the "panoramic, high-quality vision" enjoyed by long-snouted canines such as Labrador retrievers. That's why Labs like chasing balls. Pugs have a hard time seeing what's going on in the long-range department, although they're quite good at seeing what's directly in front of them.

Especially if it's a Nutty Nanner.

WHILE HUMANS ARE AWAY, THE PUG WILL PLAY

I'm not quite sure what shenanigans Ollie the Pug gets up to when we're at work. But the evidence points to a doggy equivalent of a Roman orgy.

By the time we leave for work in the morning, Ollie will have been walked, watered and fed. He'll seem relatively placid. He will either (1) lie down on a plaid quilt on the couch, or (2) sit obediently on the window seat and solemnly regard us as we walk down the garden path.

But sometimes, when we return, the house is in disarray. Ollie will have upended his cot, the one decorated with cute Dalmatian paw prints. His water dish will have been flung on its side, his chew toys scattered askew, the venetian blinds yanked into disarray.

Once Ollie gnawed a hole in the wrapped gift my daughter planned to mail to her boyfriend. Another time, he ripped up the box containing my finger-puppet collection. (Ollie, I mean, not my daughter's boyfriend.)

Perhaps such revels are the pug-dog equivalent of 1970s rock-star antics. You know, back when bands like the Who, Lynyrd Skynyrd and the Faces battled boredom on the road by trashing their hotel rooms.

But instead of flinging TV sets out the window, Ollie

the Pug merrily tears up a photo—formerly affixed to the fridge with a banana-shaped magnet—of the Chamberlains at a summer beach cabin, circa 2003. Or he ransacks the kitchen garbage bin.

Why do pets indulge in such bad craziness? It reminds me of a TV clip I once saw, provided by the owners of a wayward Lab. This dog was carefully trained not to prance about on living room couches and chairs. But its owners had a funny feeling their pet was, in their absence, breaking the all rules.

So they installed a video camera.

Just before Rover (I'll call him "Rover" to spare him public embarrassment) was left at home for the day, the dog would sit perfectly still in the middle of the living room. Nano-seconds after the door closed, he'd dash over to the window, tail wagging like a metronome. And then Rover would commence jumping on the couches and chairs like a maniac. He'd roll about, legs in the air, achieving some rarefied level of doggy nirvana.

The weirdest part is that Rover did not disrupt the arrangement of cushions on the couches and chairs.

When the front door opened upon the owners' return, Rover snapped out of his reverie, like a man roused from a three-day bender. He perched once again in the middle of the living room, unaware he'd been caught red-handed, thanks to the wonders of modern technology (not to mention the mildly disturbing paranoia of his owners).

I think Ollie the Pug is getting his jollies in a similar way. The only difference is that Ollie doesn't see fit to avoid making a mess. For making a mess is a crucial element in the Ollie the Pug pleasure-dome.

Still, it's not all fun and games. The downside of pug-dog life is constantly being ordered about by your owners. And when you go for walkies, you must always wear a leash, like Cool Hand Luke on day parole.

On the plus side, you get free room and board. You never have to go to work. Your manservant buys you special bacon-flavoured treats, regularly inserting them in your mouth to reward anything approaching good behaviour. He even pours warm water on your kibble so it's not too hard. And you get oodles of attention. Your manservant and his family continually rub your plump belly and scratch behind your ears.

Man, the last time someone rubbed my plump belly, "Love Rollercoaster" topped the hit parade and all my friends were wearing three-inch platform shoes. Oh, it's a dog's life all right.

WHY OLLIE THE PUG IS
A BETTER LISTENER
THAN I AM

The Associated Press just reported on a poll suggesting one-third of pet-owning women believe their pets are better listeners than their husbands. And 18 per cent of husbands say their pets are better listeners than their wives.

Certainly, this isn't the most uplifting of news. After all, pets don't really understand what we humans say, aside from the odd word. So if you complain to your dog about how your boss really doesn't understand you, all Ruffy will comprehend is: "Ruffy blah blah blah blah blah bah ... OK, let's go walkies."

I'm not sure if Ollie the Pug is a better listener than I am. My wife sometimes has conversations with him.

But Ollie mostly gazes back blankly, sometimes cocking his head if a particular word is particularly high-pitched.

Admittedly, when it comes to spousal confabs, my own listening skills are less than stellar. This is likely because, in my line of work, one must listen to others spout off all day.

Me: "Tell me more about your tuba, Mr. Jones."

Mr. Jones: "Well, blah blah blah blah. Blah, blah, blah. OK, let's go for walkies."

Anyway, suffice it to say journalists do plenty of dedicated listening. And one cannot let one's mind wander; one must be keenly attentive. At least, that's the theory.

So, upon returning to hearth and home, I allow that part of the brain that pays attention to others a well-deserved rest. Instead, I exercise the put-up-your-feet, drink-a-glass-of-wine, watch-silly-shows-on-TV part of the brain.

In the AP story, a woman named Christina Holmdahl admits she talks "all the time" to her cat, two dogs or three horses.

"[It is] whoever happens to be with me when I'm rambling," she was quoted as saying. "A lot of times, I'm just venting about work or complaining about my husband."

I asked my wife whether I am a good listener.

"Pretty good," she said. "Sometimes."

"Better than Ollie the Pug?" I asked.

"Um, let me think about that," she said.

It is true that sometimes, when she is telling me about her working day, I pay less than full attention. My mind drifts. I might start dreaming up sure-fire money-making ideas no one else has thought of. For instance, you know those elementary school kids who keep nervously jiggling their knees? How about strapping them to electronic devices to convert their annoying jiggles into valuable green energy?

And then, in mid-conversation, my wife will say, "Hey, are you even listening to me?"

"Yes, of course," I say.

"Then what am I talking about?"

"Your work. Work stuff."

"Specifically what about my work?"

"Well, work-related problems. Moral and philosophical dilemmas. A variety of dire situations."

Actually, the more I think about it, the more I can understand why my wife enjoys speaking to Ollie the Pug.

Sometimes, when I'm listening to her, my day-dreaming is halted by an attention-getting key word or phrase. Then I am all ears. Such words/phrases include "ran down the hall buck-naked and laughing," "would you like another drink?" and "insisted he had absolutely no idea how a light bulb could end up there."

The AP story told how some guy called Bill Rothschild enjoys talking to his crayfish. The crayfish's name is Cray Aiken. Rothschild said talking to Cray Aiken is preferable to talking to his wife because "she doesn't listen worth anything."

Unlike Bill's spouse, my wife is a good listener. She's that rare sort of listener who pays attention, then offers supportive comments.

Actually, this is somewhat annoying, as it puts me in a very bad light.

So I'm glad Ollie the Pug is helping me take up the slack. And the good thing is, dogs never gossip. So if Ollie hears something untoward about yours truly, it's no biggie. After all, pug dogs tell no tales.

YOU KNOW IT'S TIME FOR AN INTERVENTION WHEN...

Instead of being helpful around the house or writing great novels, I often spend my evenings watching stupid TV programs. One of my favourites is *Intervention*.

Intervention is a reality show in which drug addicts, alcoholics and other unfortunates stagger about, generally annoying people. They're then ambushed by the interventionist—usually a guy with a rat-face or an enormous moustache—who simultaneously lectures them and cajoles them into hopping a plane for a 90-day rehab stint.

The other night I founded myself dreaming about *Intervention*. But in the dream, it wasn't me on the hot-seat. It was Ollie the Pug.

It went something like this.

Me: "Hey, where's my cheese sandwich? I thought I left it on the table."

Ollie: "I dunno man."

Me: "Because I could swear it was right here a minute ago."

Ollie, slipping on his Ray-Bans: "Yeah ... well."

Me: "Hey. Is that a piece of cheddar hanging out of your mouth?"

Ollie: "What? No ... I mean yes! Yes, yes, yes! For God's sake, get off my friggin' back!"

Me: "Ollie, you've got to get a handle on this compulsive eating thing. It's getting out of control. It's an addiction."

Ollie: "Whatever, dude."

Later that day, Ollie the Pug and I go for walkies.

Me: "Ollie, please stop dawdling. Hey, wait a second. What's that you're chewing?"

Ollie: "Huh? Oh, nothing. It's nothing, man."

Me: "Because it really looks like a discarded Starbucks frappuccino cup."

Ollie: "It's just … you know. Just a leaf. Like a maple leaf."

Me, grabbing it: "It is a Starbucks cup. Ew. You've been licking the leftover foam!"

Ollie: "No, man … I mean, yes, yes! For God's sake, get off my friggin' back!"

That evening, I notice remnants of dried sardines scattered on the kitchen floor.

Me: "Hey. What is all this stuff?"

Ollie: "I dunno man. That's a real head-scratcher."

Me: "It looks like sardines. Hey, have you been into the dried sardine bag?"

Ollie: "Dried sardines? Dude, I haven't had a sardine for weeks."

Me: "Because it really looks like someone's been into the dried sardines. See here? The bag's all ripped."

Ollie: "Oh yeah? Now that I think of it, there was some guy in the kitchen. Yeah. And he looked like he was eating stuff."

Me: "Oh, really? You mean to tell me you saw a sardine burglar?"

Ollie: "Yes, yes. A sardine burglar. And then he ... um, ran off after eating a whole bunch of sardines right out of the bag. He ran off laughing. Weird."

Me: "Ollie ..."

Ollie: "OK man. It was me. I ate the sardines. For God's sake, get off my friggin' back!"

The next day, Ollie believes he is attending his final interview for a documentary about addiction. In fact, he is going to his intervention.

Ollie, opening the door: "So anyway, I saw this foxy lookin' terrier, and I says to her ... Hey. Just a second. What is this?"

Rat-faced interventionist: "You've got some people here who care very much about you, Ollie."

Ollie: "Oh, God. I'm outta here."

R-F interventionist: "Will you accept the gift of help we're offering you today?"

Ollie: "Will I what? Hey, did you know your face looks like a rat's face?"

Me: "Ignore him. That's just the sardines talking."

The dream ends with Ollie in an airplane, staring balefully out the window, on his way to Shady Oaks Rehab in Florida. The odd thing was, when I woke up, my fingers smelled faintly of sardines.

I told my wife about the dream. She says it's a sign that the increasingly chubby Ollie must go on a diet and exercise program. Stay tuned.

Adrian Chamberlain (not pictured) is an award-winning arts writer for the Victoria Times Colonist, the daily newspaper in Victoria, B.C.. Raised on Gabriola Island, he has a bachelor of arts degree in English from the University of Victoria and a master of arts degree in journalism from the University of Victoria.

He has won three B.C. Newspaper Awards for arts writing. In 2005 his short story, Temple Baptist, 1973, was a winner in Monday Magazine's summer fiction contest.